Demographics

Demographics
A Guide to Methods and Data Sources
for Media, Business, and Government

Steve H. Murdock
Chris Kelley
Jeffrey Jordan
Beverly Pecotte
Alvin Luedke

Paradigm Publishers
Boulder • London

Copyright © 2006 Paradigm Publishers

Published in the United States by Paradigm Publishers, 3360 Mitchell Lane Suite E, Boulder, CO 80301 USA.

Paradigm Publishers is the trade name of Birkenkamp & Company, LLC, Dean Birkenkamp, President and Publisher.

Library of Congress Cataloging-in-Publication Data has been applied for.

Printed and bound in the United States of America on acid free paper that meets the standards of the American National Standard for Permanence of Paper for Printed Library Materials.

10 09 08 07 3 4 5

Hard Cover ISBN: 1-59451-177-2

To George and Mary;
Sheryl, Curran, and Siobhan;
Angi, Jonathan, and Rachel;
Delores and John;
Becky, Alton, and Alice

Contents

List of Figures

List of Boxes

Preface

Demographics is a term that is increasingly familiar to the public and part of the essential lexicon for members of the media, human resource specialists, and public- and private-sector managers at all levels. Nearly everyone is familiar with the general term: that of the size and characteristics of a population that affect a population's use of, its participation in, and/or its access to specific types of goods and services. Thus, one commonly hears that a particular television show is intended to reach a specific demographic, that various markets for goods and services are intended for specific demographic niches, that the workforce will age and become increasingly diverse.

Despite such familiarity, it is often difficult for those who are not professional demographers to locate and effectively use demographics. How does one find data on workforce characteristics, on the number of persons with specific income levels, and on the related consumer expenditures, service usage, or tax revenues related to specific population segments? When one locates such data, they are often conveyed in technical terminology and in terms of mathematical and statistical rates that are alien to lay users.

This work attempts to address such issues for the nondemographer professional. Its purpose is to provide a single-source reference book that explains basic demographic concepts and widely used methods and that describes the basic sources for specific types of demographic, economic, and other socioeconomic and service information. It provides examples of data use and misuse and provides specific guidance for the use of demographics in news stories, in the administration of personnel programs, in the analysis of market areas and segments, in facility and fiscal planning and location analyses, and in numerous other areas.

This work is intended to serve a wide range of professionals, such as reporters with a demographic beat, human resource professionals responsible for EEOC compliance or pension fund projections, marketing analysts completing site locations, segmentation, and other analyses for clients, business managers of both for-profit and nonprofit organizations who wish to make fact-based decisions, and students in college and continuing education courses. The volume is also intended as a supplementary text for courses in media analysis, marketing analysis, and methods of business management, as well as for basic applied and undergraduate demography and social science research methods courses.

Reflecting the attempt to reach a wide audience of users, the authors are also a diverse group. We include university professors and researchers who teach courses in this area, data specialists who work directly with data users from across the nation, and a media analyst who has used demographic data for more than 25 years. What binds us together is that we are all engaged in the use of demographic data and methods with a variety of private- and public-sector users and by the fact that we are involved in extensive demographic research and other activities with businesses in the areas of personnel management, labor force analyses, organizational management, and business marketing and location analyses.

As with any work on data sources and uses, this volume will inevitably be an incomplete source on data and methods for some users. It is simply impossible, given the bourgeoning number of sources and uses, for any one volume to be anything but incomplete. We hope we have been relatively inclusive, however, and for those who do not find what they are looking for in this volume, we advise them to keep searching for their best source of information and the most appropriate ways dto use such information because there is a wider range of readily available sources than ever before. We hope for the users of this volume that we have at least provided a place to start, a beginning point for locating and using data.

We wish to thank those who have assisted us in the preparation of this work. We thank the Institute for Demographic and Socioeconomic Research and The University of Texas at San Antonio that provided support for the work. We also wish to thank numerous individuals, including Dr. Don Warren who assisted in proofing and reviewing several sections of the work, David Wang who recalculated rates for use in Chapter 3, David Donovan who helped us refine our index, and Sheila Dos Santos-Dierking who read the entire text and made useful comments that improved several sections. We especially thank Andrea Chrietzberg who carefully typed and retyped different versions of the manuscript and Charla Wright-Adkins who helped us finalize the text. We owe special appreciation to Patricia Bramwell who ensured that all parts of the preparation process were completed in a timely manner and who always managed to keep us working harmoniously even during periods of substantial stress. Finally, we express our utmost appreciation to Karen White who carefully edited the entire manuscript, seamlessly merged the work of diverse authors into an integrated document, and ensured not only consistency and accuracy in the work but also its readability.

In preparing this work, the authors have also benefited from the work of many others whom we cite throughout the text. Others to whom we owe a special debt of gratitude cannot be cited because they are so numerous, and many are unknown to us by name: those who, in requesting demographic data from us and using it for their purposes, have helped to inform and educate us in the methods and forms of data use. We thank all of them and hope at least some of them will be rewarded by finding in this volume a source that will help them in locating and effectively using data in their current and future endeavors.

Chapter 1

Introduction: Demographics in the Media, Business, and Government

This is a volume dedicated to helping readers learn how to locate and effectively use demographic and related data. It is intended for use by members of the media, human resource specialists, marketing specialists, public- and private-sector managers at all levels, and beginning students in demography and social science courses who use demographic data and techniques to address specific issues and needs. But what is demography and demographics and how are they used in the professional and applied worlds? In this introductory chapter, we begin by defining what we mean by demography and demographics and by delineating what is and what is not included when we use such terms. We then provide a brief overview of what the text will examine, and we conclude with a description of the specific organization of the remainder of the text and the limitations of the work.

What Are Demography and Demographics?

Demography and the derivative term, *demographics*, are increasingly familiar to us all, and nearly everyone is familiar with the general connotation conveyed by, these terms. For example, we commonly hear that a particular television show is intended to reach a specific demographic group, that various markets for goods and services are intended for specific demographic niches, or that the workforce must come to more adequately reflect the characteristics of the population of a region or the nation. Similarly, in the media, interest in demographics has come to play an increasingly important role in many types of reporting (see Box 1.1).

As we begin our discussion here, however, it is essential to present a more complete and technically correct definition. Demography is usually defined by the professional as the study of the size, distribution, and composition of populations; the processes determining these—namely fertility, mortality, and migration; and the determinants and consequences of all of the above (see Bogue 1968; Murdock and Ellis 1991). Demographers sometimes further differentiate between "formal demographers," who specifically focus on the demographic processes and the technical measurement of these factors and their implications for populations, and "social demographers," who stress the effects of demographic factors on other social, economic, and nondemographic factors. Others may differentiate between the pure or basic-science demographers, who seek knowledge of demographic factors and their impacts for knowledge's sake, and the "applied demographers," who use such information to address pragmatic questions.

1

Box 1.1: Demography in the Media

Consider these headlines featured in recent issues of leading newspapers and news weeklies in the U.S.:

"Flow of illegal immigrants to U.S. unabated"

"2030 forecast: mostly gray"

"Smaller percentage of poor live in high-poverty areas"

Once considered the domain of the pocket-protector crowd, issues related to demography are now a mainstream staple for news consumers.

Immigration, same-sex marriage, social security reform, prison populations—they're all fuel for interest in demography, the study of human population and its structure and change.

And when stories pertain to demographics—understanding what people think, what they are willing to buy, and how many fit this profile—interest levels soar.

Demography is a descriptive and predictive science. Demographics is an applied art and science. In both cases, the objects of study are the characteristics of human populations.

And when humans are the subject, other humans are sure to follow.

In the case of demography, the characteristics being studied tend to emphasize biological processes such as population dynamics; demographics is also concerned with a wide range of economic, social, and cultural characteristics.

Certainly, the demographer's work isn't simply to indulge the curiosity of the masses. However, serious analysis by the media of populations, patterns, and institutions has made for front-page news:

- In the political and judicial arena, subjects such as voting, representation and redistricting, jury selection, criminal justice, and prison populations have all made headlines.
- In the education arena, educational attainment, enrollment, and school redistricting are regular staples for news columns and airwaves.
- In the economic arena, subjects such as labor force, retirement, gender and race and income inequality are hot topics as are those in the family arena, such as living arrangements, commute times, and health providers.

Indeed, stories that feature a real person's life experience—a face behind the numbers—serves the public's need and desire to know about forces affecting their lives.

Journalist William Dunn (1992:191), author of *Selling the Story*, calls this bringing the numbers to life. "By delving into the grassroots repercussions of demographic trends and citing real-life examples, you can make the data understandable and palatable to readers and listeners who are eager to know how trends will affect them."

That doesn't mean reporters get the story right all the time. Mathematics is a chronic problem in the journalism field. Since numbers are at the heart of demography and demographics, the correction columns of U.S. newspapers attest to the pressure-filled rush to meet deadlines. There are often sweeping generalizations drawn from specific cases, exaggeration, and use of inappropriate data to quantify something.

Conclusions drawn from numbers are often "spun" by so-called experts pushing an agenda. The shade and tone of a story, in which the highlighting of one set of factors or statistics over another, can also lead to garbled and "misinformed" information.

News media reports involving demography generally can be categorized two ways: popular and important. Important stories are rarely popular because they tend to showcase crucial issues society does not want to face. Popular stories are rarely important because they most often are reduced to "info-tainment"—fodder for crossword puzzles.

Some of the most popular and important demographically based stories in the media emerge from the U.S. Census Bureau. A census generates news of historical significance. After all, an old joke goes, it was a census that brought Mary and Joseph to Bethlehem.

Interest in the census stems from how the numbers have changed—that is, their variance. Variance is news. Walter Lippmann (1965:216) noted this in the early twentieth century when he said, "The more points . . . at which any happening can be fixed, objectified, measured, named, the more points there are at which news can occur."

Some recent data releases by the U.S. Census Bureau illustrate the point. Indeed, the Bureau has become adept at generating news (and justifying the importance of the Census Bureau):

- Texas Becomes Nation's newest "Majority-minority" state, Census Bureau announces (Aug. 11, 2005)
- Nation adds 3 million people in last year; Nevada again fastest-growing state. (Dec. 22, 2004)
- Florida, California, and Texas to dominate future population growth, Census Bureau reports. (April 21, 2005)

News organizations often take Census Bureau news releases and attempt to localize them for their readers and viewers. Newsrooms devoted to news Web sites will often go the extra mile and create databases from census data releases so that readers may search and find just the information they're looking for. Indeed, the Census Bureau's Web site is bookmarked on many reporters' favorites list.

One of the more popular features provided by the Census Bureau is the "special report" issued on holidays.

Take Halloween of 2004. The Bureau estimated the number of potential "trick-or-treaters"—5 to 13 year olds—at 36.8 million. Who knew?

And how many potential stops could trick-or-treaters make at housing units occupied year-round? 106 million.

And where are "some places around the country that may put you in the Halloween mood?" How about Transylvania County, N.C. (29,406 residents) or Tombstone, Ariz. (population 1,547) or Skull Creek, Neb. (population 296).

Box 1.1: Demography in the Media *(continued)*

As interesting as such information might be, there are far more important demographically based stories to report. Just ask members of Congress, whose districts in the U.S. House of Representatives are subject to change (or elimination) following U.S. Census population measurements. Indeed, some of the most important issues of our time—social security, welfare reform, voting patterns, transportation, environmental policy, and federal aid to cities and states based on population—are key subjects of study for demographers and news consumers.

In the end, the best expression of a worthwhile media story about demography may well have been written by British mathematician Ian Stewart (1987:3) in *The Problems of Mathematics.* If for "mathematics" you substitute "demography" (or whatever specialized subject you're reading), you'll find some pretty sound advice not only for consuming media but also for creating it. "Tell us what the problems are, where they come from, how they get solved, what the people who solve them are like, what you can do with the answers when you've got them, what problems haven't been solved yet, how solving them or failing to solve them changes people's views of what [mathematics] is and where it's going."

The content topics studied by demographers may be best explained by examining Figure 1.1 derived from Murdock and Ellis (1991:7). As is evident from an examination of the items in this figure, demography not only examines the basic factors of population change and the fertility, mortality, and migration processes that produce such change, but also spans a large number of related substantive issue areas such as aging, family, and household patterns; changes in socioeconomic factors such as income and education; and changes in the industrial and occupational composition of an area's workforce.

Despite the obvious breadth of topics covered by professional demographers, the term *demographics* has an even wider meaning. Demographics is a nontechnical term generally used to connote information and data on the size, geographic distribution, and characteristics of a population that affect its use of, its participation in, and/or its access to specific types of goods and services. It involves the examination of how demographic factors affect such things as the markets for goods and services, school enrollment, the best location for a commercial facility, or the identification of the appropriate populations for labor force recruitment.

The forms of analyses being examined in this work obviously fit within the realm of the social and applied forms of demography. Although some technical issues will be discussed as they are used in applied areas, readers wanting more technical explanations should refer to more specialized texts (see, for example, Siegel and Swanson 2004; Siegel 2002).

Figure 1.1:   Major Variables/Dimensions in a Demographic Analysis

---

- population size

- population change

- mortality

- fertility

- migration (both national and international)

- population distribution (relative to metropolitan and nonmetropolitan areas; central cities and suburbs; rural and urban areas; by the population size, density of settlement, and among blocks, tracts, etc. of an area)

- compositional characteristics
  - age
  - sex/gender
  - race
  - ethnicity
  - marital status (including never married, married, separated, divorced, and widowed)
  - household and family types (including family and nonfamily households and family and nonfamily households by age, sex, race/ethnicity, and marital status of householder [head] and presence and/or number of children)
  - educational status (both years and degrees completed)
  - employment by
    - status (employed, unemployed, or underemployed)
    - occupation
    - industry
  - income, wealth, and poverty
  - socioeconomic status (summative measures using income, education, and occupational variables).

Source: Murdock and Ellis 1991:7.

What Will Be Examined in this Text and Why?

Despite increasing familiarity with the term *demographics*, those who are not professional demographers often find it difficult to locate and effectively use demographic and related information. How do you find data on workforce characteristics; on the number of persons with specific income levels; and on the related consumer expenditures, service usage, or tax revenues related to specific population segments? When are data on a demographic characteristic too old to use and when is it better to use older rather than more recent data? When you do locate such data, it is often provided in forms and conveyed in technical terminology and in terms of mathematical and statistical rates and forms that are unfamiliar to lay users. What specifically is meant by a crude birth rate or by life expectancy and life span? What is a cohort-component demographic projection? What is the difference between household and family income? What are the ways that you can tell how reliable data are likely to be and thus how safely one can use them in an important news story or market analysis? How do you write clearly and effectively about demographic data? What are the best ways to graphically illustrate demographic information (for example, charts, tables, graphs)? What are the most effective ways to communicate written and graphic information for written reports and for newspapers, television, radio, and the Internet?

This text attempts to concisely address such issues for the nonprofessional demographer in a single source reference book that, (1) explains basic demographic concepts, terms, and methods widely used in descriptions of groups, areas, and markets; (2) describes the basic sources for specific types of demographic, economic, and other socioeconomic and service information at a variety of geographical levels; (3) provides guidance and examples of how to efficiently, effectively, and appropriately use demographics in news stories, in the administration of personnel and other programs, in the analysis of market areas and segments, in location analyses, and in other forms of media, business, and management analyses; and (4) presents examples of the location and application of such data in the media, business, and government.

This text fills a niche between the technical information available in applied demography texts that stress more advanced statistical methods (Murdock and Ellis 1991; Siegel 2002) and those volumes that are largely listings of sources and methods of analyses for specific issues and/or professional groups, such as the media (see for example, Bass 2001; Weinberg 1996; Kovach and Rosentiel 2001; Meyer 1972); marketing and advertising (Lazer 1997; Pooler 2002); management (Tsui and Gutek 2000); or business in general (Pol and Thomas 1997; Kintner et al. 1995).

This text differs from sources such as those above in three primary ways. First, it provides a general guide to sources that is relatively generic and thus of greater utility to the general analyst who works in multiple areas. It is likely to appeal to the increasing number of journalists and business analysts who work in multiple beats and business enterprises and to managers of profit and nonprofit organizations. Second, its section on how to effectively use such data is relatively unique. All of the above noted sources either provide a guide to sources or present methods for analysis in specific areas. General principles for data use are often largely ignored, and thus these works often do little to provide the readers with general guidance that can assist them in working with many different types of data. Finally, this text is unique in its comprehensive coverage of printed and Internet sources; its description of basic methods for data manipulation and use; and its explanation of materials, methods, and applications through easy to understand examples. We hope that such features ensure that the text will occupy a niche that will make it of substantial and unique value to readers.

Organization of the Text

This text consists of nine chapters, including this introduction, divided into four parts. The four parts examine (1) the basic concepts and methods of demographic analyses; (2) the major sources of demographic and related data; (3) principles and methods for the effective and appropriate use of demographic data and information; and (4) examples of the use of demographic data and methods in the areas of media, business, and government. Each of these parts, and each chapter within, is written as a stand-alone segment that can be mastered by the reader without reading the rest of the text. Thus, this text can be used as a reference source to address specific questions as well as used as a more complete source for obtaining a wider understanding of the subject matter.

The first part examines concepts, terms, and methods. It introduces the reader to those basic demographic concepts that are likely to be encountered in reading demographic materials. Even more importantly, it provides readers with an introduction to sources that can be consulted to find the correct definitions for areal units (e.g., blocks, tracts, metropolitan and micropolitan areas), variable and term definitions (e.g., households, families, sub-families), forms of data (e.g., micro-data and aggregate data), and similar factors. Finally, this part introduces the reader to basic demographic methods and measures for examining such factors as population change, fertility, mortality, migration, population distribution and concentration, and demographic characteristics. This part is one that both conveys basic knowledge of the content of demography and provides readers with the knowledge of where to go to find out what they do not know as well as how to present data and the results of simple analyses with basic widely used measures.

The second part of the work provides an overview of secondary governmental and private-sector data sources. It includes an introduction, not only to such basic sources as the U.S. Bureau of the Census, the U.S. Department of Labor, the National Centers for Health Statistics and Educational Statistics, the U.S. Department of Justice, and others, but also to selected private sources such as Dunn and Bradstreet. In addition to describing the types of data items available, their frequency of production and availability, and the contacts for obtaining these data, it provides a relatively comprehensive guide to Internet sources and to systematic techniques for mining Internet data sources. After reading these chapters, the reader should know where to locate different types of data and how to extract and use them.

The third part is intended to provide guidance to the reader in three areas. First, the reader will learn how to correctly identify and use data items. In this part of the work, emphasis is placed on how to identify the specific data item desired, how to ensure its definitional and geographic consistency if it is measured across time, and how to determine the likely accuracy of sample-based data items. A second part of this section concentrates on how to evaluate the reasonableness of data items collected. It stresses the importance of comparing data values obtained to those for similar population groups, in similar areas, and relative to predominant trends in regions, states, and the nation. It also provides a basic overview of those trends that can assist the reader in knowing what to expect and what types of patterns will contradict expectations.

The final substantive chapter of the work brings to life the concepts, data, and methods discussed in previous sections by demonstrating the use of sources, appropriate methods for item identification and use, and basic methods. Examples are provided from the media, from marketing, from personnel evaluation and labor force analyses, and from business and governmental management. In each example, the purpose is, not only to demonstrate how to locate appropriate data items, but also how to make the key decisions about the quality of data and its appropriateness to the geographic area in question and how to summarize it to correctly and succinctly convey the information required to address a particular issue. This part serves to convey the interrelated nature of the information provided in earlier parts and the utility of the integrated use of this information.

The work concludes with a summary chapter that provides a brief synopsis of major points presented in the work and outlines areas of additional information and methods that the reader may wish to pursue. It ends by stressing that any such source is but an introduction to the sources and uses of demographic data and by providing the reader with a description of other sources that should be consulted to expand knowledge of each of the areas covered in the text.

The work also contains several appendices. Appendix A presents a glossary of commonly used demographic terms and measures that can be referred to as a quick source to refresh the reader's memory about specific measures. Appendix B lists helpful Internet sites devoted to demographic methods, sources, and communication resources. Appendix C presents an essay for government, business, and demographic professionals on effective ways to work with the media. Appendix D provides a companion essay for media professionals on effective ways to work with government, business, and demographic professionals.

Limitations of the Work

The work attempts to provide a relatively comprehensive, yet measured and understandable, guide to the sources and uses of demographic data for the applied analyst who is attempting to describe and/or make pragmatic decisions. As such, it attempts to walk the fine line between being so general as to be little more than a listing of inadequately explained items and methods and being so specific and detailed that comprehension of its contents requires a level of statistical and mathematical expertise that is beyond that which should reasonably be expected of its intended user. We hope we have been successful in walking that line.

The work is nevertheless clearly limited in several ways. It is, at least in some ways, incomplete simply because no single source can ever address all of the data sources and forms and methods of use likely to be required by the professionals in the wide range of areas likely to be represented by the users of this work. It is limited by the fact that, although the authors have attempted to present sources of data and methods of use that extend to many disciplines, they are obviously not experts in all of these areas and so the uses suggested may in some cases be naive. It is also limited in that by attempting to meet several needs it is clearly not specialized in any one of them. It is not a comprehensive reference to all sources of all types of demographic data, it does not provide a comprehensive overview of demographic methods, it does not claim to adequately describe all of the potential forms of use or misuse of analytical data or techniques of analysis. Due to space and other limitations, including the knowledge base of the authors, it admittedly provides only a partial view of the rich amount of data and increasingly sophisticated techniques available for analyzing such data. We hope, however, that it is both sufficiently rich in data and methods and sufficiently helpful in teaching readers how to effectively use and present data and avoid inappropriately using data that it will serve as a useful ongoing reference source.

Chapter 2

Basic Concepts, Definitions, and Geography of Demography

As with any area of study, it is essential in demography to understand its basic concepts and the definitions of its key terms and to become familiar with the types of geographic areas for which demographic data are generally available. Knowing the jargon of demography and knowing the types of areas for which data can be obtained are essential first steps in knowing how to effectively use its data. In this chapter, we provide an overview of key concepts and definitions and examine the geographic bases used in demography and its applications.

Basic Dimensions and Processes

Given the definition of demography as the study of population size, distribution, and composition and of the processes that determine these, a logical place to begin in understanding demographic factors is to understand (1) what is meant by a population; (2) the three key dimensions of population–size, distribution, and composition; and (3) the three basic processes that determine population change–fertility, mortality, and migration.

A **population** refers to the persons living in a specific area at a specific point in time. It refers to the aggregate, the group of people as a whole, in an area. As such, it has characteristics that are unique to an aggregate and are not just the sum of individuals' traits or characteristics. For example, a population can have a death rate, birth rate, etc., but individuals are either alive or dead, have or have not been born. There is no death or birth "rate" for an individual. Demographers tend to concentrate on the description of factors about the population as a whole, as an aggregate.

Size refers simply to the number of people in the population in a given area, **distribution** to how the people in a population are distributed across space (with space usually being defined as a specific type of area such as a metropolitan area, city, census tract, etc.), and **composition** to the characteristics of the population (e.g., age, sex, race/ethnicity). **Fertility** refers to the reproductive behavior (specifically the number of births) in a population, **mortality** to the incidence of death in a population, and **migration** to the movement of people from one area to another.

Unlike fertility and mortality that are clearly identifiable from a biological event, a migration event is less directly observable. Migration is not simply movement but relatively permanent movement from one area to another. Thus commuting is not considered migration. The exact definition of migration varies

11

among nations. In the United States, migrants are those who have changed their residence from one county to another. There is no minimum distance required to be a migrant.

Migration is often further differentiated relative to its source and its relationship to an area of reference. Thus migration includes both **domestic migration,** which is the movement of people into or out of an area from or to another area in the same nation, and **international migration,** which is the movement of people from or to other nations (also referred to by the general term of **immigration**). Relative to domestic migration, movement of people into an area of reference is referred to as **inmigration**, movement out of an area of reference is referred to as **outmigration,** and the net result of inmigration and outmigration is referred to as **net domestic migration**. When describing immigration, the movement of persons into a reference nation is referred to by the general term **immigration**, the movement of people out of a reference nation is referred to as **emigration,** and the net result is referred to as **net immigration**.

Populations change due to fertility, mortality, and migration. This process of change is frequently represented by what is referred to as the population equation or bookkeeping equation of population: $P_{t2} = P_{t1} + B_{t1-t2} - D_{t1-t2} + M_{t1-t2}$. This equation simply indicates that a population of an area at any later period of time is equal to the population at an earlier period, plus the births between the earlier and later period of time, minus the deaths between the two periods, plus the amount of net migration in the area between the two periods. Since net migration refers to the net difference between migration into and migration out of an area, if the number of people moving into an area is greater than the number moving out, then the value of M_{t1-t2} will be positive and a positive value will be added to the equation. If migration out of an area exceeds migration into an area, then the value of this term will be a negative, and adding a negative number means that the migration term will be subtracted from the equation. The benefit of thinking in terms of this bookkeeping equation is that it significantly simplifies understanding population change: only these three processes determine whether a population increases, decreases, or stays the same size.

Details of the Dimensions

Each of the three basic dimensions of population size, distribution, and composition has its own specialized terms and definitions. As noted above, **population size** is simply the number of people in a population of a given area. Although demographers and others often compare the populations of different areas at different points in time, it is change in population that is usually the major focus of interest. Change is most often described in percentage terms. The **percent change** in the population is simply computed by subtracting population at an earlier period of time (e.g., 2000) from a population at a later period of time (e.g., 2005), dividing the difference by the population at the earlier period, and multiplying the result by 100. For example, the percent population change from 2000 to 2005 for an area with 1,000 people in 2000 and 1,250 people in 2005 would be 25 percent. Percent changes can be computed for any period of time, but annual rates are often used to allow for easier comparison. If you know the percent population change for an area from 1990 to 2000 and you have a percent change for the same area for 2000 to 2005, annualizing the two rates often eases comparisons. In this case, you simply divide the 1990–2000 percent change by 10 and the 2000–2005 percent change by 5. In general, if demographers are describing growth rates that they are comparing across time, they do so in annualized percentages (that is, rates).

One of the factors that makes this apparently simple task more complicated is that population change is continuous (people are continuously being born, dying, and migrating); as a result, population values are always given for a specific date. For example, the decennial census in the United States is for April 1 of the year ending in 0 (e.g., April 1, 1990; April 1, 2000, etc.), but population estimates are often for July 1 of the year indicated. This middle of the year period is provided because a middle of the year value is logical for computing rates; this middle value gives an indication of the "average" number of people at risk of experiencing an event (e.g., birth, death) of interest during a calendar year. The difficulty is that if you compare census data taken from the decennial census (e.g., April 1, 2000) to data taken from an estimate (e.g., July 1, 2005) and you fail to note the difference in dates and compare your percentage to an annualized rate for a previous period, such as the annualized rate from the 1990 census (April 1, 1990) to the 2000 census (April 1, 2000), you can end up comparing a percentage growth for 1.25 years to one for 1.0 year. This frequently made mistake often occurs when the first post-census estimates are reported. It can be avoided by making sure you always check for the reference date in the data for which comparisons are being made.

One of the ways that rates of population change are examined in order to determine long-term impacts is in terms of the time necessary for a population to double in size. Although this "doubling period for the population" is discernable by solving a relatively simple equation, it is even simpler to think of it in terms of what is sometimes referred to as the **rule of 70**. If you divide the annual rate of population growth into 70, you obtain the number of years at that rate of growth that it will take to double the population. For example, a population growth rate of 2.0 percent per year doubles a population in 35 years, a rate of 1.5 percent per year doubles a population in roughly 47 years, and a 1.0 percent rate of growth doubles the population in 70 years.

Population distribution indicates how the members of a population are distributed over a given unit of space. The unit can be any geographic area from nations to census blocks. In the case of legally or statistically formed areas, such as counties or metropolitan areas, comparisons generally are not differentiated in terms of the difference in the physical size of the unit even though the land area covered may vary substantially.

If you are interested in how many people are living on a given unit of land, measures such as density are often used. **Population density** is the number of people per square mile. In international statistics, density is usually computed as persons per square kilometer or hectare.

In still other cases, demographers are interested in how different types of people are distributed across the same space. For example, the segregation of racial/ethnic groups is often examined in terms of residential segregation, and such segregation is usually measured by statistical measures that examine the similarity in the relative percentage of two populations living in a given set of geographic units (such as census tracts or blocks). For example, if the residential patterns of Blacks and Whites are being compared across a common level of geography (such as tracts) and 90 percent of Blacks live in one subset of tracts in a city while 90 percent of Whites live in another largely nonoverlapping subset of tracts, these two populations are said to be highly segregated. Measures such as the **Index Of Dissimilarity** and the **Gini Coefficient** (described in the next chapter) generally have values between 0 and 1, with values closer to 1.0 indicating higher levels of maldistribution (i.e., segregation) between the populations.

The **composition of a population** describes its characteristics. The most commonly described characteristic in demographic analyses are those shown in Figure 1.1. Below we briefly define each of these and discuss some common uses of them.

Age is among the most important demographic and social factors. Age determines everything from legal rights (e.g., you must be 18 years of age or older to vote in the United States), to the likelihood of experiencing certain events (e.g., the probability of dying increases with age), to the social expectations that are placed on members of a population. For example, a person in the United States is expected to marry in his or her late teens or 20s and to raise children as a young and middle aged adult. Age also tends to be closely associated with other characteristics. For example, persons are more likely to be in school at ages less than 25, to be at their peak earnings power and to be home owners when they are middle aged, and to be retired at older ages. Commonly used names are also used to describe specific age groups. **Youth** are generally those less than 18 years of age, the **elderly** are those 65 years of age or older (occasionally 60 years of age is used to define the elderly), the **dependent** are those who are too young or old to work (usually those who are less than 18 and those who are 65 years of age or older in a developed country and those who are less than 15 and those who are 60 or 65 years of age or older in a developing country).

Particularly important in demographic analyses is the concept of a **cohort**. A demographic cohort is a group of people born during the same time period and potentially having other common characteristics. Demographers examine how people born during a certain time period differ from those born at different time periods. The baby boom generation, generations X and Y, and other popularly used labels are really demographic cohorts. In addition to being of the same age, other common characteristics may form the basis for a cohort. For example, you can examine the cohort born between 1946 and 1964, the cohort of males born during this time period, the cohort of Black males born during this period, the cohort of Black male college graduates born during this period, etc.

Because the effects of common birth years may actually involve the effects of several types of factors that are closely associated with persons from a given birth period, demographic analysts often attempt to separate the effects of three related dimensions. When examining the behaviors or perspectives of people by age, it is important to know whether these behaviors and perspectives are a result of their age (and would be similar for any persons reaching that age at any point in time) or the time period in which they are being examined (the actual calendar period or year[s] involved), or whether the results are the effect of these persons having been born in a specific period and coming to adulthood during a time when specific historical, social, or economic events occurred. For example, if in 2001 a survey of persons 85 years old or older indicated that they had substantial concern about their financial status, it would be important to be able to identify what part of their concern was a result of the decline in the economy in 2001 (the period effect), what part was due to their advanced age and related dependency (the age effect), and what part was due to the fact that they came of age during the Great Depression and, as a result, had always been concerned about changes in the economy (the cohort effect). Although the techniques for separating these three types of effects are more statistically complex than can be briefly discussed in this work, it is important to be aware of such differences.

Sex or gender is an important demographic factor because one key process, births, is experienced only by females and also because there are important differences in mortality; in the forms and types of morbidity experienced, in historical occupational and industry patterns of employment; and in income, poverty, and other socioeconomic factors. Some of these differences (the role of sex in fertility, mortality, and morbidity) appear to be a product of biological factors (i.e., sexual differences) while others (such as differences in occupational distributions and income) appear to be a product of the social, cultural, and economic differences experienced by males and females (i.e., gender differences). In most cases, an examination of demographic differences will include analyses of sex or gender differences.

Race and **ethnicity** are concepts that are often confused and this confusion is further compounded when information on ancestry and country of birth is provided. As used in the U.S. Census of Population and Housing, all designations of race and ethnicity are self-identified by respondents to the census. They are not verified by the census taker. Race is determined by a question that asks the respondent to indicate whether he or she and every other member of the household is White, Black or African American, Asian, American Indian or Alaskan Native, Native Hawaiian or Pacific Islander, or a member of some Other racial group. Ethnicity is determined from a separate question that asks the respondents to indicate for themselves and all other members of the household whether they are of Hispanic origin or not of Hispanic origin. If the respondents are of Hispanic origin they are further asked to indicate the specific Hispanic group (e.g., Cuban, Puerto Rican, Mexican-American, or Other Hispanic) of which they and each other member of the household are a member. Hispanic is not a race category nor do White, Black, etc. refer to ethnic categories. Race and ethnicity are different dimensions derived from responses to different questions. Because many people think of ethnicity in the same way as they do race, demographers may create a mixed set of categories by using Hispanics as a single group and subtracting Hispanics from the race groups on the basis of the race of Hispanics, thus creating a set of non-Hispanic race categories that are exclusive of Hispanics. When this separation is done, it is possible to create a set of race/ethnicity groupings that are mutually exclusive and sum to the total population. What further complicates understanding race and ethnic differences is that the 2000 Census was the first to allow respondents to indicate that they came from more than one race category. Although this was an important step in allowing persons of mixed race to accurately describe their racial heritage, it meant that there were 63 race combinations for Hispanics and non-Hispanics (i.e., 126 total categories). Although only about 2.5 percent of the U.S. population indicated two or more race combinations, alternative ways of combining racial/ethnic groups means that it is essential to know how an analyst has combined racial/ethnic groups.

Two other data items are sometimes used in conjunction with race/ethnicity. **Ancestry** simply refers to which country or countries a person traces his or her heritage. This census question does not differentiate respondents by their time in the country, so that among different populations, the number claiming any given ancestry is likely to vary substantially. Much less variable is the item **country of birth**. **Foreign-born** persons are first-generation immigrants, and by using this category in combination with other variables, country of birth has been useful in identifying important characteristics of immigrants, such as their legal status (see Passel 2005).

Marital status refers to whether someone is currently single (including never married and widowed), married or separated, or divorced, as indicated by prevailing laws in the state of residence. Rates for such factors are usually computed on the population 15 years of age or older since most states prohibit marriage at very young ages.

Household and **family** status are closely related but separate concepts. A **household** consists of all people living in the same housing unit, with a **housing unit** being defined as a separate unit. There are two forms of households, **family**

and **nonfamily**. A **family household** is one with two or more persons who are related by kinship, marriage, or adoption; a **nonfamily household** consists of a single person or two or more unrelated persons living in the same housing unit. All families are households but not all households are families. Family households are often further differentiated between married-couple and single-parent households, and single-parent households by the sex of the householder (i.e., male or female householder families). Such distinctions are important in the use of many other data items. For example, nonfamily households and single-parent households usually have lower incomes than family households because they are less likely to involve two working adults. Similarly, median or mean family income is usually higher than household income because household income includes single person and other nonfamily households that generally have lower incomes. It is critical to note such differences in describing the characteristics of a household. How a society puts itself together in groups to live has major socioeconomic as well as social implications.

Educational status refers to the level of education in a population and is usually defined in terms either of educational attainment levels or years of school completed. Attainment levels refer to formally recognized educational degrees or milestones so that comparisons between areas are often made on the percentage of persons completing high school, percentage completing college, etc. Years of education are also used for such comparisons, although years are often interpreted in terms of the normal number of years necessary to complete a certain level of attainment (e.g., 12 years to indicate completion of high school, 16 for completion of a baccalaureate degree).

Employment status refers to whether people are **employed** or **unemployed**, with the sum of the employed (including those in the armed forces) and unemployed making up an area's **workforce**. Defining these terms is more complicated than it might appear, however, because employment means that a person is employed in a job, but it does not mean that the person is employed for a given period of time during a month. Being employed does not mean you are employed full-time: a person may be employed full-time (generally defined as working 30 or more or 35 or more hours per week) or part-time (generally consisting of employment of less than 30 or 35 hours per week). Even more difficult to understand is that for a person in the United States to be considered as **unemployed**, the person must not only not be employed but must also be looking for work within the past month through a state unemployment office. A person who is no longer looking for work or who is not looking through the assistance of formal channels is simply not counted. Such persons are sometimes referred to as discouraged workers, but they will not generally be included in official employment or unemployment estimates.

Industry and **occupation** are also of importance for understanding the economic characteristics of an area. In general, **industry** refers to the **type of**

business a person works for and **occupation** to **what a person does** in that business. Industry categories such as farming, manufacturing, government, and service are the types of activities performed by the organization for which a person works. Occupations are activities that are done for such organizations, such as manager, laborer, skilled crafts person, etc. Because the occupation in which a person is able to be employed is usually dependent on the person's level of education, experience, and other factors, occupational status is often useful in identifying how well a person is likely to be doing economically.

Key measures of economic well-being are the variables of income, wealth, and poverty. **Income** refers to money received from any source such as employment, investments, pensions, etc. Several measures of income are commonly used, including aggregate income, per capita income, mean income, and median income. **Aggregate personal** or **household income** refers to the total income of all persons or households in a population. Since it is dependent on the number of people or households, employment, and other factors about an area, aggregate income is not very useful for comparisons across areas, but it does provide some indication of the total monetary resources of a population. **Per capita income**, which is often used to measure income, is obtained by simply dividing total aggregate personal income by the number of people in the population. So constructed, it allows for more meaningful comparisons across areas than aggregate income.

Mean (household, family, etc.) income is the numerical average of all households' or families' incomes in an area–or simply, the sum of all incomes of all households or families in an area divided by the number of households or families with income in that area. The problem with the mean income measure is that it can be misleading if there are extreme values among those being averaged. For example, if there were three households in a population and one made $10,000 per year, a second $17,000 per year, and the other made $1,000,000 per year, the mean household income would be about $342,000 per year, a value that does not accurately estimate the resources available to any of the three households in the population. **Median (household or family) income** is more frequently used. The median is the value that divides a ranked income distribution in half. If there is an odd number of income observations it will be the value of a specific person or household, but if there is an even number of observations it will be the average of the two that divide the middle. In the above example, the median income value is $17,000. Although this is the exact value for only one of the three income observations, it is clearly more representative of the income of two of the three households than the mean. If the example had included a fourth observation, for example a household with an income of $20,000, the median income of the four-household population would have been $17,000 plus $20,000 divided by 2, or $18,500. This value would again be more representative for more observations (in this case for 3 of 4) than the mean value. Finally, it is very important to know what sources of income are being included in an income measurement. Does the measure include retirement benefits? Does it include just wage or salary income, or does it also include investment income? It is very easy to end up with income values that are simply not comparable if you do not carefully check the types of income included in a given definition.

Poverty is a measure of the lack of income. Poverty levels generally refer to the number of persons/families/households living with incomes below a certain level. This level was originally developed as a measure of the minimum resources that it would take for a person/family/household to pay for the most basic services relative to food, shelter, and transportation. The "poverty level" is continuously updated by the use of cost-of-living data from the Bureau of Labor Statistics and varies by the size of the household and the age of persons in the household. What is most often quoted is the poverty level for a family of four, but it is important to recognize that there are separate values for a single-person household and households of other sizes as well. **Poverty rate** is the percentage of households in poverty among those for which poverty status is determined (i.e., with incomes below a given level). Poverty for subpopulations are also often quoted, such as the poverty rate for children or the elderly. In these cases, it is the poverty rate of households with children or with an elderly person that is being referred to, since most children and some elderly people will not have direct incomes.

Wealth is less often used but provides a wider indication of the total resources available to a household than income alone, and may be particularly important in describing the resources available to certain groups (such as the elderly). It refers to all of the assets possessed by a household, including the value of personal possessions and the value of property including homes, businesses, savings, stock, bonds, income, etc. As with income, you must carefully check what is included in any given description of assets or wealth. Data on wealth are now more frequently collected than in the past and can provide a more complete picture of resources available to an individual or household. Such data also often demonstrate even greater disparities between households with specific characteristics than data on income alone.

Finally, in all matters related to dollars and the examination of trends in income, wealth, and other economic factors examined over time, it is essential to know whether change is being computed in **constant** or **current** dollars. In constant dollar calculations, the income or related monetary values for a given year are taken as the standard and dollars for all other time periods are adjusted to be in reference to the dollar values for the selected year. This adjustment is made by removing the effects of inflation on the values for all years between the selected base year and the other years of interest. By so doing, direct comparisons can be made in what are termed "real" or "constant" versus "inflated" or "current" dollars. If this adjustment is not done and current dollars are used for each period, it will be impossible to discern whether an apparent change in income between two periods (such as 2000 to 2005) shows a real change in the resources of the group for which income data are being collected or whether the change is simply the result of inflation. The ready availability of price and wage inflation ratios (inflators and deflators) from the Bureau of Labor Statistics makes this a relatively simple calculation and one that can significantly increase the information value provided by financial data.

Geography of Demography

Demography studies population, and population refers to a group of people living in a given area–a given geographic area. Knowing the geographic referents for demographic analyses, like knowing definitions and concepts, is essential to having a basic understanding of demographics. The basis of geography for demographic analysis in the United States is census geography, or the geography used in the decennial censuses by the U.S. Bureau of the Census. The Census uses both administrative areas as defined for governmental purposes, such as incorporated towns and cities, counties, states, and the nation as a whole, and statistical areas to ensure the utility of census data. Census statistical geography is hierarchical; that is, each larger unit subsumes all smaller units and each larger unit is composed of multiple smaller units. The smallest unit of census geography is the **census block**. In urban areas a block is (in common usage) an area bounded on each of its four sides by different streets. In rural areas, blocks may be larger in geographical terms and are drawn to reflect clearly identifiable boundaries or features. There are no population size criteria for blocks. The entire country is blocked for purposes of the census. The next level, the **block group,** is composed of a set of blocks; the number of blocks in a block group varies depending on geographic characteristics (roads, water systems, etc.) and population size of census blocks, but in general block groups range in size from 500 to 3,000 people with an optimal size of 1,500 people. Groups of block groups are combined to form **census tracts**. Census tracts vary in size from 1,000 to 8,000 and average about 4,000 people. All other areas use combinations of these three levels of geography or these plus certain administrative units.

One widely used area delineation is that for **metropolitan statistical areas (MSAs)**. These consist of groupings of counties that have a central city county with a central city of 50,000 or more people. Counties will be designated as part of a metropolitan area if a minimum of 25 percent of their workforce commutes to the central city county for work or 25 percent or more of the jobs in the county are held by residents of the central city county. These counties are commonly referred to as suburban counties. Metropolitan areas are named using a specified set of conventions, with the largest city within the metropolitan area being the first name in the official name and other names being used if they meet certain size criteria. All remaining counties that are not part of metropolitan areas are referred to as nonmetropolitan counties. Although these nonmetropolitan counties are not necessarily rural in terms of the rural-urban definition noted below, they have often been used as a simplistic means of defining rural counties. With the post-2000 Census changes, a new classification of area was also designated in the delineation of metropolitan areas: the **micropolitan statistical area**. Micropolitan areas consist of a county with at least one urban cluster with between 10,000 and 50,000 people and adjacent counties with high levels of social and economic interaction with the core as measured through commuting. These definitions differ slightly in New England states. In all cases, however, it is essential to check MSA definitions because such areas are periodically redefined.

Rural and **urban** areas are often perceived in terms that are very different from the way that they have been officially defined. Prior to 2000, urban areas consisted of all places (towns and cities) with 2,500 or more people, and rural areas were all other small towns and open country areas. Even under this definition, there was no such thing as a rural or urban county. In 2000, "rural" and "urban" were redefined to eliminate any place referent, and density alone was used to designate urban and rural areas. Using census blocks as the basis, urban areas have been defined as all blocks with a population of at least 1,000 persons per square mile, and rural territory as all blocks with densities below 1,000 persons per square mile, but with one exception. Under certain conditions, blocks with a density of less than 1,000 but more than 500 persons per square mile were also designated as urban if they were adjacent to other urban blocks. This drastically different definition has made comparisons of 2000 rural and urban areas to those for earlier periods virtually impossible. As a result, we do not recommend comparing the rural and urban parts of areas before 2000 to such areas as defined in 2000 or later.

There is one final set of census areas that must be mentioned. In the 2000 and earlier censuses, a sample of individual respondent households that had completed the detailed census questionnaire (what is described below as the long-form items) was selected and provided as a data source for use in detailed analyses. Whereas census data are commonly provided only for aggregates (populations of people from census statistical or administrative areas), these sample data are for individual households (and persons within them) and are referred to as the **Public Use Microdata Sample (PUMS)**. Microdata is the term the census uses for all such samples that include actual individual households' surveys. The advantage of these samples is that analyses of multiple combinations of characteristics can be done, and the analyst's examination is not limited to those combinations included in census summary data files. For example, if you wanted to know how many households in an area had children and also had incomes of more than $100,000, lived in housing units worth more than $200,000, and had a householder who was less than 40 years of age, you can estimate the results from PUMS. No such "cross-tabulation" capability is provided in the regular census summary files. The major limitation of these data is that they are not collected for standard census geographies because of the need to ensure that the identity of individual households is protected.

The areas for which such data are available are areas drawn by state-level experts in each state (using Census guidelines) and are referred to as PUMS Areas or PUMAs. These areas have a minimum of 100,000 persons for the five percent sample and a minimum of 400,000 persons for the one percent sample. For these areas, one percent and five percent samples (of all households in the area completing the long-form part of the census) are available.

Some areas of relevance for business and other applications may or may not reflect census areas. Examples include trade areas, market areas, and service areas. In most cases, data on actual customers' residences are used to establish exact addresses that may then use related census areas' data to examine population characteristics. In analyses for other products, including many media products, market areas may be largely coterminous with census areas such as metropolitan areas. The census may provide data useful in drawing the boundaries of these areas, but it makes no attempt to construct such areas for analysts.

Conclusions

In this chapter basic demographic concepts, definitions, and geographies have been described. These are only the basics. If you need more detailed information you should consult additional sources. As a basic short introduction to the field of demography, we recommend *Population: A Lively Introduction* by McFall published in 2003 by the Population Reference Bureau. It provides, in a relatively few pages, a good overview of what demographics is all about. We have also included an appendix in this publication that provides definitions of key demographic terms (Appendix A). In addition, an excellent source of definitions relative to U.S. Census and similar publications can be obtained by examining the appendices for census products. Nearly all printed and Web-based forms of census works include one or more appendices that provide definitions of terms and of the geographies examined in the work. We suggest that these appendices be referred to in all instances in which you are using a census data item or area type that is unfamiliar to you. If you cannot find the definitions in the source you are using, consult the Web site for the United States Bureau of the Census [http://www.census.gov/], which has excellent technical definitions of terms and geographies. Examining Web sites is also useful for obtaining important definitions in materials from most other federal and state agencies that provide technical information.

In sum, demography is like all other areas—you must start with and know the basics. This chapter has provided an introduction to these basics. In the chapters that follow, we attempt to assist the reader in building upon that base, but as with all technical areas, an important limitation to recognize is that no one knows it all. Even the most experienced demographer constantly encounters new data items and an ever changing set of technical materials.

Chapter 3

Basic Demographic Measures and Methods

In this chapter, we examine several general methods and measures used in basic demographic analyses.[1] Basic knowledge of them is essential to users wishing to understand the results of demographic analyses. We begin with several general measures and then discuss measures for individual demographic concepts and variables.

General Measures

Use of Rates

Among the most basic measures in demography is the measurement of rates of incidence and change. Rates allow the incidence of a factor in populations of different sizes to be directly compared. Perhaps the most widely used of all measures of change is simply the percent change from one period to another. As shown in Figure 3.1, percent change is expressed as the amount of increase or decrease in population per 100 persons and is thus a rate per 100 persons in the population.

Rates are the most basic measures used to evaluate demographic factors and processes. *Rates measure the relative frequency of occurrence of an event in a population.* In demographic analyses, the most common form of a rate is simply a numerator consisting of a number of events for a given time period divided by a denominator, which is the population experiencing or exposed to the risk of the event during the same time period as the occurrence of the event. The value obtained after the numerator is divided by the denominator is then multiplied by a constant, such as 100 or 1,000. This constant places values on a common base and eliminates the need to use small decimal values.

Figure 3.1: Percent Change in Population

$$\text{Percent Population Change} = \frac{(\text{Population at } t_2 - \text{Population at } t_1)}{(\text{Population at } t_1)} = \quad \text{X} \quad 100$$

Example:

$$\begin{array}{l}\text{Percent Change} \\ \text{U.S. Population} \\ 2000\text{–}2004\end{array} = \frac{293{,}655{,}404 - 281{,}421{,}906}{281{,}421{,}906} \quad \text{X} \quad 100 \quad = \quad 4.3\%$$

Because demographic events are measured for discrete time periods and because populations change over time, both the numerator and denominator for rates are often adjusted. In the numerator, the most common adjustment is to take an average number of events for several years rather than a single year. This step is done because there can be substantial year-to-year fluctuations in the number of events, and you want to obtain a rate that indicates the "usual" incidence of an event in a population. For an area with a small number of events, year-to-year fluctuations can lead to very misleading rates if the time at which the events are measured is an unusual period.

A choice of denominators is also required. That is, rates are variously computed with denominators that are population values at the beginning of the period of interest (e.g., 1990 in a 1990-to-2000 rate), at the midpoint (e.g., 1995 for a 1990-to-2000 rate), or at the end of the period (e.g., 2000 for a 1990-to-2000 rate). When the beginning-of-the-period population is used, the rate expresses change in the event relative to the beginning population base. The midpoint population (usually obtained by using an average of a beginning and end-of-period population) is the most often used to compute basic rates and represents an attempt to measure the average number of persons at risk of the event. The endpoint population is often used to assess change relative to the population remaining after a period of change. Whatever procedure is used to obtain the numerator or the denominator, it is essential that all rates to be compared for various areas use values for equivalent time periods.

Three types of rates are commonly employed in demographic analyses. These three types of rates are *crude, general, and specific rates*. These rates are shown in Figures 3.2 through 3.4. They differ in the extent to which they measure an event relative to the population at risk of the event. That is, *a crude rate measures the occurrence relative to the total population*, only part of which may actually be subject to the risk of experiencing the event. For example, births occur only to females of certain ages, while the crude birth rate shown in Figure 3.2 measures births relative to the total population. Crude rates can be misleading if a population is composed of a disproportionate number of persons with or without the characteristics likely to lead to their experiencing the event. As the name implies, crude rates only crudely measure the frequency of occurrence of the phenomenon in a population.

General rates, such as the example shown in Figure 3.3, *more closely limit the measurement of the base denominator to those persons actually at risk of the event*. The general fertility rate shown in this figure is a rate per 1,000 women in the ages in which child-bearing is most likely to occur, 15–44 years of age. *Specific rates*, such as that shown in Figure 3.4, *show the greatest specificity, measuring events relative to the specific population at risk*. Thus, the events shown in this figure are the births to women 20–24 years of age relative to the number of women 20–24 years of age. The advantage of the use of specific rates is clearly that they

Figure 3.2: Crude Rates

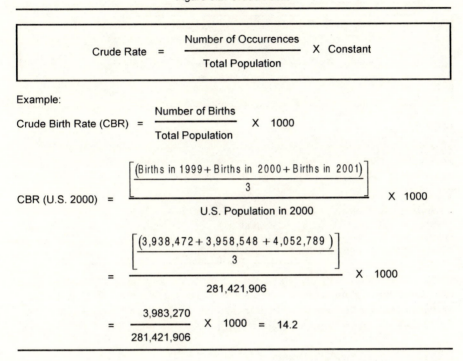

$$\text{Crude Rate} = \frac{\text{Number of Occurrences}}{\text{Total Population}} \times \text{Constant}$$

Example:

$$\text{Crude Birth Rate (CBR)} = \frac{\text{Number of Births}}{\text{Total Population}} \times 1000$$

$$\text{CBR (U.S. 2000)} = \frac{\left[\dfrac{(\text{Births in } 1999 + \text{Births in } 2000 + \text{Births in } 2001)}{3}\right]}{\text{U.S. Population in 2000}} \times 1000$$

$$= \frac{\left[\dfrac{(3{,}938{,}472 + 3{,}958{,}548 + 4{,}052{,}789)}{3}\right]}{281{,}421{,}906} \times 1000$$

$$= \frac{3{,}983{,}270}{281{,}421{,}906} \times 1000 = 14.2$$

Figure 3.3: General Rates

$$\text{General Rate} = \frac{\text{Number of Occurrences}}{\text{Population at Risk}} \times \text{Constant}$$

Example:

$$\text{General Fertility Rate (GFR)} = \frac{\text{Number of Births}}{\text{Females 15–44}} \times 1000$$

$$\text{GFR (U.S. 2000)} = \frac{3{,}958{,}548}{61{,}593{,}334} \times 1000 = 64.3$$

Figure 3.4: Specific Rates

$$\text{Specific Rate} = \frac{\text{Number of Occurrences to Persons with Specific Characteristic}}{\text{Number of Persons with Specific Characteristic}} \quad \text{X} \quad \text{Constant}$$

Example:

$$\text{Age-Sex Specific Fertility Rate (ASFR) for Women in Age Group I} = \frac{\text{Births to Women in Age Group I}}{\text{Women in Age Group I}} \quad \text{X} \quad 1000$$

$$\text{ASFR for U.S. Females 20–24 (2000)}^a = \frac{850,000}{9,258,000} \quad \text{X} \quad 1000 \quad = \quad 91.8$$

[a]Estimated from Current Population Survey, June 2000.

more exactly measure the events relative to those persons most likely to actually experience them. If the data are available to obtain specific rates, they are usually preferred because they are less likely to be misleading relative to the incidence of the phenomena in the populations of interest.

Descriptive Statistical Measures
Numerous widely used measures from general statistical analyses are also commonly applied in demographic analyses to measure the characteristics of the distribution of a variable within a population. Among these are the three measures of central tendency, the mean, the median, and the mode. *The mean, or simple arithmetic average, is widely used to measure demographic factors* (e.g., age, income, etc.). The advantage of using the mean is that its properties are well-known statistically, and associated measures, such as the variance and standard deviation and measures of statistical significance, can be used to describe the characteristics of its distribution. The mean is often replaced in general analyses with either the mode or the median because the value of the mean can be skewed by extreme cases, while the mode and median are not affected by extreme values. *The mode simply indicates the value occurring most often, while the median is the value that divides a ranked distribution in half (with 50 percent above and 50 percent below the median value).* Which of the three measures should be used depends on the nature of the distribution and the norms of use in an analytical area. The median is normally used to describe age and income, the mean to describe such factors as age at first marriage, and the mode to refer to such factors as the most common occupation of employment in an area. Other descriptive statistics and procedures

such as histograms, graphs, charts, frequency distributions, etc. are also widely used. You must develop a basic knowledge of general statistics as well as knowledge of methods unique to demography to accurately use demographic data.

Measures of the Major Demographic Processes and Variables

Measures of Population Change

In addition to the percent change measures, there are several other widely used measures of population change based on different ways of measuring change over time. The most common measure is based on the exponential change formula. It assumes continuous compounding, thus simulating the constant additions (through, births and inmigration) and deletions (through deaths and outmigration) that occur in populations. This measure is shown in Figure 3.5. When population growth rates are quoted, it is generally this rate that is being referenced.

As noted in the preceding chapter, one widely used means of describing rates of change is in terms of the number of years it would take for an area to double its existing population at its present rate of change. By solving the exponential formula for time (t) in years with the population set at double its existing size (that is, at 2P), the formula produced shows that the *doubling time can be determined by dividing the rate of change per year into 0.6932*. When an alternative (geometric) growth rate is computed the 2P value is 0.6968. This is the basis for the rule of 70 referred to above.

Measures of the Demographic Processes

The three demographic processes of fertility, mortality, and migration use many of the general measures noted above as well as several unique measures. Crude, general, and specific rates are widely used to describe the processes. The three rates shown in Figures 3.2 through 3.4 are the rates most often used to measure fertility. The number of births used in the values is obtained from vital statistics departments in state departments of health or from the National Center for Health Statistics, with births being those by the place of residence of the mother (rather than place of occurrence). For mortality and migration, crude and age-specific rates are used with both applying to such events by place of residence. Since all persons are subject to the risk of death and of migrating, however, there is no counterpart to the general rate for mortality or migration.

Fertility Measures. In addition to the crude, general, and specific fertility rates shown in Figures 3.2 through 3.4, one additional measure will be examined here. This is the *total fertility rate* shown in Figure 3.6. *It is the sum of the age-specific fertility rates for all women in the child-bearing ages, and, when adjusted to be per-person-specific, indicates the number of children that the average woman would have in her reproductive lifetime if she aged through her reproductive years exposed to the age-specific rates prevailing at a specific point*

Figure 3.5: Exponential Rate of Change

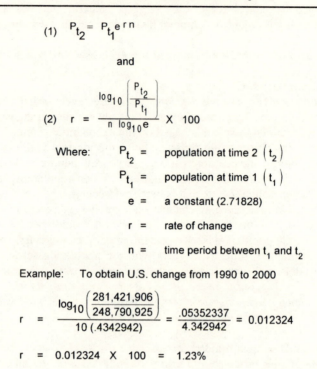

(1) $P_{t_2} = P_{t_1} e^{rn}$

and

(2) $r = \dfrac{\log_{10}\left(\dfrac{P_{t_2}}{P_{t_1}}\right)}{n \, \log_{10} e} \times 100$

Where: P_{t_2} =   population at time 2 $\left(t_2\right)$

P_{t_1} =   population at time 1 $\left(t_1\right)$

e =   a constant (2.71828)

r =   rate of change

n =   time period between t_1 and t_2

Example: To obtain U.S. change from 1990 to 2000

$r = \dfrac{\log_{10}\left(\dfrac{281,421,906}{248,790,925}\right)}{10 \, (.4342942)} = \dfrac{.05352337}{4.342942} = 0.012324$

$r = 0.012324 \times 100 = 1.23\%$

in time. In the example shown in Figure 3.6, the rate indicates that the average woman would have had 2.017 children during her reproductive lifetime. Among the most widely discussed levels of total fertility is the rate of 2.1, referred to as the replacement rate of fertility. This is the total fertility rate that is necessary for a population (with survival rates similar to those of the United States) to replace itself because the average woman must replace both herself and her mate. The value required for replacement is slightly larger than 2.0 because some women do not survive to reproductive age or do not bear children.

Mortality Measures. In addition to the crude death rate and age-specific death rates delineated above, the measurement of the incidence of death in a population tends to center on the incidence of deaths at certain ages, on the causes of death, and on the effects of a given set of death rates over the life-cycle of a population.

Death rates among infants are of particular interest because infant mortality is often indicative of the general level of health care in a society and because the death rate is higher during the first year of life than for any other age prior to about

Figure 3.6: Total Fertility Rate (TFR)

$$\text{Total Fertility Rate} \ = \ (N_i) \ \sum_{i=15-19}^{i=40-44} ASFR_i \times 1000$$

Where:

i = age group

$ASFR_i$ = age-specific fertility rate for age group i

N_i = number of years in age group i

Example:

	Age		ASFR[a]
	15–19	=	59.7
For 2000 for	20–24	=	91.8
the United States	25–29	=	107.9
	30–34	=	87.9
	35–39	=	45.1
	40–44	=	10.9
	Σ	=	403.3

TFR   =   403.3 x   5   =   2016.5

TFR per woman   =   2.017

---

[a]Estimated from Current Population Survey, June, 2000.

---

age 55. Figure 3.7 presents three widely used measures of infant deaths. *Infant mortality is simply the number of deaths occurring to persons less than one year of age.* Since persons less than one year of age are those born during the last year, the number of infant deaths is divided by the number of births to obtain the infant mortality rate. *The infant mortality rate is also often examined in terms of two components, deaths to infants less than one month old, referred to as the neonatal death rate, and deaths to infants one month to one year of age, referred to as the post-neonatal death rate* (see Figure 3.7). The reason for the use of these two rates is that deaths to infants less than a month old are often related to problems in gestation and to such factors as the level of prenatal care received by the mother during pregnancy. Post-neonatal mortality is likely to reflect post-birth environmental factors rather than problems related to gestation.

Because different causes of death are more likely to occur to persons in certain ages and to persons with different socioeconomic characteristics, there is

Figure 3.7: Selected Measures of Infant Mortality

Infant Mortality Rate (IMR)

$$\text{IMR} = \frac{D_{0-1_i}}{B_i} \times 1000$$

Where: D_{0-1_i} =   deaths to persons less than one year of age during year i

           B_i =   births during year i

Neonatal Mortality Rate (NMR)

$$\text{NMR} = \frac{D_{<1 \text{ month}_i}}{B_i} \times 1000$$

Where: $D_{<1 \text{ month}_i}$ =   deaths to persons less than one month of age in year i

           B_i =   births in year i

Postneonatal Mortality Rate (PNMR)

$$\text{PNMR} = \frac{D_{1-12 \text{ months}_i}}{B_i} \times 1000$$

Where: $D_{1-12 \text{ months}_i}$ =   deaths to persons one month to less than one year of age in year i

           B_i =   births in year i

---

also considerable interest in the incidence of deaths by cause. *The cause-specific death rate, defined as the number of deaths from a given cause in an area divided by the population of the area,* is commonly used. Such analyses generally show coronary disease and cancer to be the major causes of death in nearly all areas of the United States.

Among the most unique techniques used to measure the impacts of mortality is the set of procedures referred to as life-table analysis. *Life-table analysis is a procedure that simulates the impacts of a given set of age-specific mortality rates on a population over the entire lifetime of the population.* It simulates how many persons would die at each age until the last person in the population dies. A hypothetical population of 100,000 (called the radix) is used with elements of the table computed for each age. Figure 3.8 provides an example of a life table and Figure 3.9 briefly defines the standard elements of a life table. The prefix before these elements and the x suffix after them refer respectively to the

Figure 3.8: Abridged Life Table for the Male Population of a Hypothetical Area, 2000

Age Interval (in Years) x to x+n	Proportion Dying In Interval $(_nq_x)$	Number Living at Beginning of Age x (l_x)	Number Dying During Interval $(_nd_x)$	Number of Person Years Lived In Interval $(_nL_x)$	Total Person Years Lived in This and All Subsequent Ages (T_x)	Average Number of Years Remaining Life at Beginning of Age x $\overset{o}{e}_x$
0–1	0.01152	100,000	1,152	98,951	7,534,601	75.35
1–5	0.00214	98,848	212	394,891	7,435,650	75.22
5–10	0.00129	98,636	127	492,824	7,040,758	71.38
10–15	0.00140	98,509	138	492,227	6,547,934	66.47
15–20	0.00465	98,371	457	490,918	6,055,707	61.56
20–25	0.00630	97,914	617	487,996	5,564,789	56.83
25–30	0.00695	97,297	676	484,829	5,076,793	52.18
30–35	0.00779	96,621	753	481,298	4,591,964	47.53
35–40	0.00908	95,868	870	477,297	4,110,666	42.88
40–45	0.01155	94,998	1,097	472,468	3,633,369	38.25
45–50	0.01741	93,901	1,635	465,666	3,160,901	33.66
50–55	0.02913	92,266	2,688	455,019	2,695,235	29.21
55–60	0.04756	89,578	4,260	437,671	2,240,216	25.01
60–65	0.07326	85,318	6,250	411,594	1,802,545	21.13
65–70	0.10299	79,068	8,143	375,391	1,390,951	17.59
70–75	0.15271	70,925	10,831	328,630	1,015,560	14.32
75–80	0.22217	60,094	13,351	267,759	686,929	11.43
80–85	0.31761	46,743	14,846	196,598	419,170	8.97
85+	1.00000	31,897	31,897	222,572	222,572	6.98

Figure 3.9: Elements of a Life Table

x to x + n	=	the period of life between two exact ages (x and x + n where n = age interval).
$_nq_x$	=	the proportion of the persons in the age group alive at the beginning of an indicated age interval (x) who die before reaching the end of that age interval (x + n).
l_x	=	the number of persons living at the beginning of the indicated age interval (x) out of the total number of births assumed as the radix of the table.
$_nd_x$	=	the number of persons who die within the indicated age interval (x to x + n).
$_nL_x$	=	the number of person-years lived within the indicated age interval (x to x + n) by all persons from age x to x + n.
T_x	=	the total number of person-years lived after the beginning of the indicated age interval.
$\overset{o}{e}_x$	=	the average remaining lifetime (in years) for a person who survives to the beginning of the indicated age interval. This is also referred to as life expectancy.

size of the age groupings being examined and to the initial age (x) of the age group being considered (e.g., $_{15}L_{19}$ would refer to the number of person years lived during the five-year interval x to x + n where x is 15 and the interval n is 5, hence $_{15}L_{19}$).

Life tables vary in form and in coverage. Complete life tables are computed for single years of age from 0 to 1, 1 to 2, etc. to some terminal age, such as 85 years of age and older. An abridged life table uses 5-year or some other set of multiple-age categories. Life tables may also examine only the effect of rates of transition from life to death (in which case they are referred to as *single-decrement life tables)*, or the effects of mortality and one or more other factor(s), such as labor force participation, first marriage rates, or school enrollment rates (in which case they are referred to as *multiple-decrement life tables)*.

The elements of a life table (see Figure 3.9) show key factors about a population. The two most important are the $_nq_x$ factor, which is the probability of dying during a given age period (given the death rates prevailing at a given point in time), and the $\overset{o}{e}_x$ factor, which is the remaining years of life at a given age. The $\overset{o}{e}_x$ factor for age 0 is the life expectancy at birth and is commonly referred to simply as "life expectancy."

The life table is a useful procedure for discerning how any type of population (of anything) that decreases over time to 0 is impacted by different rates of death or failure. It is widely used in the actuarial sciences where probabilities of dying are one factor used to determine premium rates for the insurance industry but also for discerning such factors as the failure rate for different types of manufactured products (Siegel 2002).

Migration Rates. Migration is a difficult process to measure in the United States because there is no direct registration system (as in some nations) that requires residents of the United States to indicate when they change residences. Migration must be measured primarily with data from the decennial census, from periodic surveys, or by indirect methods. In the decennial census, migration is measured by asking respondents their place of residence five years ago. If their residence at the time of the census and five years earlier are different, respondents are considered to have moved, but if the respondent's residence at the time of the census and five years earlier are in different counties (or countries), the respondent is then considered to have migrated. As noted in Chapter 2, persons are considered to have inmigrated or outmigrated from the standpoint of a given area, while the difference between inmigration and outmigration for an area is referred to as net migration. Figure 3.10 shows several rates commonly employed to measure migration.

Migration is usually measured using what are referred to as residual methods. These methods are equivalent to solving the bookkeeping or population equation for the migration component. Thus, the amount of total population change attributable to births and deaths is accounted for and the remaining difference between the total change and that due to births and deaths–the residual–is assumed to be due to migration. Figure 3.11 shows the net migration formula for computing residual measures of net migration.

It is critical to remember that a residual net migration measure uses a residual, not a direct, measure as the estimate of migration. It requires the assumption that all of the residual is due to migration. In fact, the residual difference may also include such nonmigration factors as differences in the coverage in the counts of the population in the two successive periods, errors of various types in reporting or analyzing data, etc. If the existence of such additional factors is known, the factors should be eliminated before the rate is computed. Since other factors affecting the residual are usually not known and cannot therefore be eliminated, it is essential to recognize the limitations of residual migration measures.

Measures of Population Distribution

Measures of population distribution attempt to identify how a population is distributed relative to the physical space or land area its members inhabit. Among the most often used measures of population distribution are simply the percentages or proportions of persons in different types of areas, such as metropolitan or nonmetropolitan, rural or urban, cities and towns versus open country, and in places of different population sizes. Another widely used measure is *the average number of persons per unit of land* (usually square miles) referred to as *population density*.

Figure 3.10: Migration Rates

$$\text{Inmigration rate} \quad = \quad \frac{I}{P} \quad \times \quad k$$

$$\text{Outmigration rate} \quad = \quad \frac{O}{P} \quad \times \quad k$$

$$\text{Net migration rate} \quad = \quad \frac{I - O}{P} \quad \times \quad k$$

Where:
I = inmigrants
O = outmigrants
P = population
k = constant

Figure 3.11: Residual Net Migration Rate (NMR)

$$NMR_{t_2} \quad = \quad \frac{\left(P_{t_2} - P_{t_1}\right) - \left(B_{t_1 - t_2} - D_{t_1 - t_2}\right)}{\tfrac{1}{2}\left(P_{t_2} + P_{t_1}\right)}$$

Where:

P_{t_1} = population at an earlier period of time (t_1)

P_{t_2} = population at a later period of time (t_2)

$B_{t_1 - t_2}$ = births between t_1 and t_2

$D_{t_1 - t_2}$ = deaths between t_1 and t_2

Figure 3.12 shows the standard measure of density with an example for the United States in 2000.

  Several other measures of population distribution (that are also used to measure other demographic factors) are shown in Figures 3.13 through 3.15. Figure 3.13 describes the *population potential* measure, which provides a "relative" measure of population distribution relative to two or more specific geographic sites. It indicates the number of persons for whom each of several alternative geographic locations is the most accessible. In the example in Figure 3.13, the population potentials of areas 1 and 2 are compared. These areas could be census tracts, blocks, counties, or any other geographic unit, and any number of units could be compared. In this example, the distances shown are the distances between the area of interest (i.e., area 1 in the top panel and area 2 in the bottom panel) and each of the other

Figure 3.12: Population Density

$$\text{Population Density} = \frac{\text{Total Population}}{\text{Land Area (square miles)}}$$

Example:

Population
Density in $= \dfrac{281,421,906}{3,537,438} =$ 79.6 persons
the U.S. in   per square mile
2000

Figure 3.13: Population Potential

$$\text{Population Potential at } L_o \text{ (Location)} = \sum_{i=1}^{n} \frac{P_i}{D_i}$$

Example:

Area 1

Area	Population (P)	Distance (D)	P/D
1	50,000	3 miles	16,667
2	60,000	8 miles	7,500
3	10,000	2 miles	5,000

Total Population Potential for Area 1 = 29,167

Area 2

Area	Population (P)	Distance (D)	P/D
1	50,000	8 miles	6,250
2	60,000	2 miles	30,000
3	10,000	5 miles	2,000

Total Population Potential for Area 2 = 38,250

areas. Usually the distance is measured from the center of one area to the center of the other. The distance shown for the reference areas for which the population potentials are being measured (i.e., the 3 miles shown for area 1 in the top panel and the 2 miles shown for area 2 in the bottom panel) is the average distance a person in the reference area would have to travel to reach the reference point in the area (usually this is the center of the area). In this example, area 2 has a larger population potential than area 1 and is thus accessible to a larger number of persons than area 1.

The population potential and related measures are often used in site selection analyses. If you are considering several alternative sites for a commercial or public-service facility, you can use this measure (adjusting for physical features, transportation, and other factors) to determine which of several sites is the most accessible to the largest number of persons. The basic formula is used with its components restricted to the items of interest. For example, population may be replaced by households or by households or persons with given purchasing capabilities, incomes, or other characteristics. Distance may be replaced by travel time to the site or other relevant factors. This measure is easily computed using procedures incorporated in many standard geographic information systems and in many other widely available software packages.

Figures 3.14 and 3.15 show several other widely used measures of population distribution. The top panel of Figure 3.14 provides a table containing a set of data for a hypothetical set of areas. The first three columns of this table show five population size categories of areas (column 1), the total population accounted for by all areas in each category (column 2), and the number of individual areas in each population size category (column 3). The first row of data for these items shows that there was one area in the size category of 50,000 or more persons that had 80,000 persons, row 2 shows that there were two areas in the size category with 20,000 to 49,999 persons that together had 90,000 persons, etc. Columns 4 and 5 show the simple percentage distributions of population and areas. That is, the first row of data indicates that areas of 50,000 or more persons accounted for 40 percent of the total population (of 200,000) in the areas (column 4) and for 10 percent of the areas (of 10 areas) included in the table (column 5). Columns 6 and 7 show the cumulative percentage distributions, cumulating from the largest to the smallest size of place categories. Ten percent of all areas was in the 50,000+ category, another 20 percent, or a cumulative percentage of 30 percent, was in places in the 50,000+ plus the 20,000–49,999 category (column 7). Forty percent of the population was in places of 50,000+, another 45 percent in places of 20,000 to 49,999 for a total cumulative percentage of 85 percent of the population in areas of 50,000+ plus areas of 20,000 to 49,999 (column 6).

The Lorenz Curve shown in the bottom panel of Figure 3.14 shows a graphical representation of the two cumulative percentage distributions (columns 6 and 7) relative to one another. This curve was constructed by connecting points that indicate the proportion of population relative to the proportion of areas with a line drawn through the points and connecting the two ends of the diagonal line. In this example, 10 percent of the places accounted for 40 percent of the population, 30 percent of the places for 85 percent of the population, etc. The diagonal line is provided as a base for comparison because it represents the condition in which the two cumulative percentage distributions would be identical (e.g., 10 percent of the areas would have 10 percent of the population, 20 percent of the areas would account for 20 percent of the population, etc.).

The distance between the diagonal line and the curve constructed from the cumulative percentage distributions of the two factors shows how dissimilar the percentage distributions of the two factors are given the size categories shown. The greater the distance between the diagonal line and the curve, the greater the difference in the distributions of the two factors. This curve may be drawn either above or below the diagonal depending on whether the cumulative distributions are cumulated from the highest to the lowest category or from the lowest to the highest. For example, the curve in Figure 3.14 would have shown the same area between the diagonal and the curve had the percentage distribution shown in the table been cumulated from the smallest to the largest population size category (i.e., from the bottom up rather than from the top down), but the curve would have been above instead of below the diagonal (so computed, 40 percent of the areas or places would have accounted for 5 percent of the population, and 60 percent of the places would have accounted for 10 percent of the population, etc.)

The Lorenz Curve is widely used because it presents an easy-to-construct graph of the relationship between any two cumulative percentage distributions. For example, it is often used in economic analyses to indicate the distribution of income relative to the population or the number of households and, when used as such, can be seen as a graphical measure of income inequality.

An examination of the Lorenz Curve reveals that the area between the diagonal and the curve indicates the extent of maldistribution between the two factors graphed on the two axes. The relevant measure is *the proportion of the area between the diagonal and the curve of the total area under (or over) the diagonal*. The measure of this area is called the *Gini Coefficient*. The formula for this coefficient is shown in Figure 3.15 along with an example of its use with the data in Figure 3.14. This coefficient is simply the difference in the cross products of the cumulative percentage distributions. In the example shown, the Gini Coefficient indicates that roughly 60 percent of the area under the diagonal is between the diagonal and the Lorenz Curve, indicating the population in places tends to be concentrated relative to the size of place categories.

Another useful measure of distribution is the *Index of Dissimilarity*, which indicates the similarity of two categorical percentage distributions (not cumulative, but simple percentage distributions). This measure, which *is one-half the sum of the absolute differences between the percentage values in the categories of the two distributions*, is interpreted as indicating the proportion of population that would have to change categories for the two distributions to be identical. In the example in Figure 3.15, the Index of Dissimilarity is 55, indicating that 55 percent of the population would have to change categories for the two distributions to be identical.

Both the Gini Coefficient and the Index of Dissimilarity have been extensively used to assess inequalities in distributions. The latter measure is often

Figure 3.14: Distribution of a Hypothetical Population by Size
of Place Category and the Related Lorenz Curve

Population By Size of Place Category	Total Population	Number of Areas	Percent		Cumulative Percent	
			(x_i)	(y_i)	(X_i)	(Y_i)
50,000 +	80,000	1	40	10	40	10
20,000–49,999	90,000	2	45	20	85	30
10,000–19,999	10,000	1	5	10	90	40
5,000–9,999	10,000	2	5	20	95	60
<5,000	10,000	4	5	40	100	100

Lorenz Curve

referred to as the *segregation index* (see discussion below) because it is employed to measure the segregation of racial/ethnic groups in cities and other areas. These and related measures are among the most useful for assessing how two factors are distributed relative to one another and are some of the only simple summative measures available for measuring the differences between percentage distributions of two categorical variables (see Massey and Denton 1988 for a discussion of other segregation measures).

It is important to recognize the wide applicability of these measures. They can be used in at least three ways: (1) to assess the difference between two factors for several different areas (e.g., the distribution of customers and income among market areas or the distribution of service centers relative to the number of clients for a public service); (2) to compare two different areas relative to their distribution across categories of a single variable (e.g., to compare the income distributions for two different market areas); or (3) to examine changes in the distribution of a

Figure 3.15: Gini Coefficient and Index of Dissimilarity–Measures of Population Distribution

Gini Coefficient (G_i)

$$G_i = \sum_{i=1}^{n} X_i \, Y_{i+1} - \sum_{i=1}^{n} X_{i+1} \, Y_i$$

Where: X_i and Y_i are cumulative percentage distributions for two factors

Index of Dissimilarity (ID)

$$ID = 1/2 \sum_{i=1}^{k} |x_i - y_i|$$

Where: x_i and y_i are percentage distributions for two factors

(continued)

Figure 3.15 (continued)

Example: To compute Gini Coefficient and Index of Dissimilarity given the following data:

Percentage distributions, cumulative percentage distributions, and cross products of cumulative percentage distributions for a hypothetical population (See Figure 3.14)

Size of Place Category	Percentage Distribution		Cumulative Percentage Distribution		Proportional Cross Products		Absolute Percent Difference
	Places (y_i)	Population (x_i)	Places (Y_i)	Population (X_i)	$X_i Y_{i+1}$	$X_{i+1} Y_i$	$|y_i - x_i|$
50,000 +	10	40	10	40	0.12	0.09	30
20,000–49,999	20	45	30	85	0.34	0.27	25
10,000–19,999	10	5	40	90	0.54	0.38	5
5,000–9,999	20	5	60	95	0.95	0.60	15
<5,000	40	5	100	100	–	–	35
Sum (Σ) =					1.95	1.34	110

Gini (G_i) = 1.95 – 1.34 = 0.61

Index of Dissimilarity (ID) = 110/2 = 55

variable over time (e.g., the proportion of a product's users in different income categories in two different years). These measures are not only usefully applied to examine the geographic distribution of population relative to land area, but can also be used to examine the distribution of other factors likely to be of interest to the business or government analyst.

Measures of Population Composition

Many of the general measures described at the beginning of this chapter are also employed to measure the characteristics of a population. For example, median age is a common measure of the age structure of a population, as are simple percentage distributions showing the number and percentage of persons in each age group. Similarly, median income and median years of education are widely used measures. In the following discussion of measures of population composition, only the relatively unique measures of each variable are delineated. You should be aware, however, that many of the general measures can also be usefully applied to describe the characteristics of a population.

Age and Sex Composition. The age and sex composition of a population affects many other characteristics of a population, from its rates of fertility to the nature of the goods and services it is likely to demand. Age is often measured by the use of simple percentage distributions and the mean or median years of age. Sex is similarly a key variable that is often measured in terms of the percentage of the population that is male or female. Figures 3.16 through 3.18 provide other basic measures of these two variables.

Figure 3.16 shows the *dependency ratio. This ratio indicates the number of persons in dependent ages relative to the number in the working ages.* The dependent ages are variously defined as those 0–14 or 0–19 and those 65 years of age or older, with those in the working ages being all those at ages between the young and old dependent ages. The ratio is sometimes computed separately for the young, in which case it is referred to as the *youth dependency ratio*, or for the old, referred to as the *old-age dependency ratio*. The dependency ratio indicates how a population's age structure is likely to affect its ability to support itself and is therefore used both as a measure of age and as a measure of the economic characteristics of a population. It is a measure that is widely used in the description of government programs, with the old age component frequently used in discussions of the future of social security.

Figure 3.17 presents perhaps the most widely used measure of the sex composition of the population. This is the *sex ratio, the number of males divided by the number of females and multiplied by 100*. The sex ratio is extensively used in many forms of analyses because of its consistency. In most developed countries, the sex ratio at birth is approximately 105 males per 100 females, decreasing to about 100 by age 20 to 30 and to about 60 by age 80. Wide variation from these expected levels can be used to identify areas where unique demographic events have

Figure 3.16: Dependency Ratio (DR)

$$DR = \frac{P_{0-14} + P_{65+}}{P_{15-64}} \times 100$$

Where: P_{0-14} = number of persons 0–14
                                 years of age

         P_{65+} = number of persons 65 years of
                              age and older

         P_{15-64} = number of persons 15–64
                                years of age

Example:

Texas DR = $\dfrac{4,910,004 + 2,072,532}{13,869,284}$ X 100 = 50.3
(2000)

Figure 3.17: Sex Ratio (SR)

$$SR = \frac{P_M}{P_F} \times 100$$

Where: P_M = number of males

         P_F = number of females

Example:

Texas SR (2000) = $\dfrac{10,352,910}{10,498,910}$ X 100 = 98.6

occurred. For example, some (Bean et al. 1982; 1983) have used sex ratio differences between Mexican states bordering the United States and those within the interior of Mexico to estimate the number of illegal immigrants from Mexico in the United States. In addition, the sex ratio has come to be increasingly used as a factor that is indicative of conditions likely to lead to particular patterns of behavior and family change (Fossett and Kiecolt 1990).

      One often employed technique to indicate the joint distribution of age and sex in a population is the age-sex pyramid. *Age-sex pyramids are constructed simply by taking the number of males and females of each age and graphing their numbers,* as shown in Figure 3.18, or by using percentages in which the number of

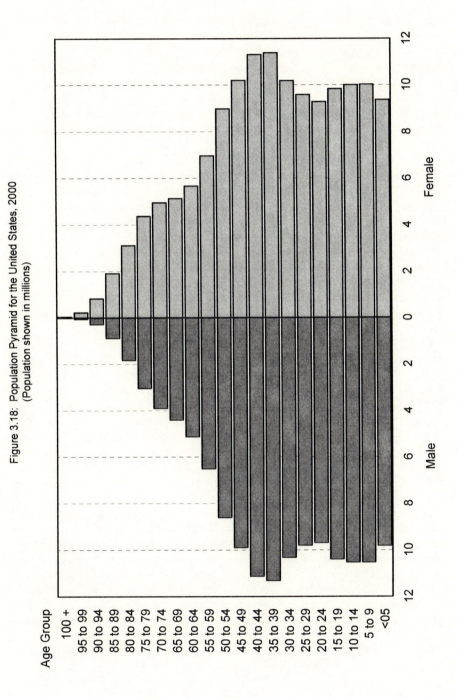

Figure 3.18: Population Pyramid for the United States, 2000
(Population shown in millions)

each sex in each age group is divided by the total population and the percentages shown graphically. By tradition, females are placed on the right and males on the left side of the pyramid. In general, it is the width of the base (beginning years) of the pyramid relative to its width at other ages that is of interest in analyzing the pyramids. Pyramids with larger bases reveal populations that are generally younger, while those with age categories that are more uniform in width are likely to be indicative of an older population. Such pyramids can be very useful for graphically demonstrating the differences in the age and sex distributions of two population groups.

Race/Ethnicity. There are relatively few unique measures for assessing the race/ethnicity composition of a population. Rather, these characteristics are usually described in terms of simple numerical and percentage comparisons of the numbers and proportions of persons in each race/ethnicity group in a population. Two measures that are used to measure the similarity in the patterns of distribution of racial/ethnic groups across geographical areas are the Index of Dissimilarity (or segregation index) and the Gini Coefficient described under the discussion of measures of population distribution. If the proportions of persons in two different racial/ethnic groups are compared for a set of areas, then the Index of Dissimilarity and Gini Coefficient measures can be computed in the manner shown in Figure 3.15. These can be interpreted as indicating the extent to which two racial/ethnic groups are physically segregated from one another. For analysts and reporters wishing to assess whether racial/ethnic groups are more likely to live in majority neighborhoods now than in the past, these can be very useful measures.

Household, Family, and Marital Characteristics. The measures of household, family, and marital composition most often used are simply the number and percentage of persons in specific categories of households and marital statuses. Other frequently used measures are *average household size (the number of persons living in households divided by the number of households)*, median or average age at first marriage, and nuptiality (life) tables showing the numbers and proportions married and single in populations with different levels of age-specific marriage and mortality rates. Household, family, and marital characteristics are measured by the use of quite general measures.

Educational Characteristics. O'Hare et al. (2004) provide measures of educational inputs into the educational system, measures of progression in the system, and measures of outputs from the system. The measures of educational input most often used are simply the crude, general, and age-specific rates of enrollment, with ages 5–34 used in the general rate. Similarly, the measures of educational output most often employed are simply the crude and age-specific illiteracy rates (with illiteracy variously defined either by measured skills or less than 3 or less than 5 or some other designated number of years of formal education) and the attainment rate, (the proportion of the population achieving a given level of education). Such retention and graduation rates can be usefully applied to measure the progress of persons through an educational system. These measures, when combined with other descriptive measures of education, such as the median years of school completed, can provide a comprehensive overview of the educational characteristics of a population.

Economic Characteristics. The most commonly used means of describing the economic characteristics of the population are such descriptive measures as median income, per capita income (which is simply the mean income per person in a population), the percentage of the labor force employed and unemployed, and the percentage employed by occupational and industrial categories. Among the other measures commonly used to describe the labor force are the labor force participation rates shown in Figure 3.19. Although labor force participation rates are widely known and used, the fact that these rates are crude, general, and specific rates of labor force participation is seldom recognized. In fact, the general labor force participation rate is commonly referred to simply as the labor force participation rate. Such rates, together with basic descriptive measures, can provide a relatively complete description of the basic economic characteristics of a population.

Controlling for Demographic Effects

Measures and methods that provide means of describing the extent and form of demographic processes and characteristics in a population have been presented above. In this section, procedures are discussed that attempt to determine how much difference demographic factors make in the determination of a pattern of events or behaviors. Viewed alternatively, analysts and other users are sometimes interested in knowing how similar patterns of events or behaviors would be in two different populations if they had the same age structure, ethnic composition, etc. For example, the sales for a given product may be less in one area than in another, and the populations of the areas may have very different age structures. Is the difference in sales due to age structure differences or to other factors? Service centers for a public service may have been established on the basis of similar total populations, but the case load in one center may be much higher than in another. Is the difference in case loads due to differences in the ethnic, household, and income compositions of the populations of the areas or due to other factors, such as differences in staff interpretations of regulations? In a reporter's comparison of the increase in the number and percentage of married-couple households in different areas, what role might be played by differences in the ethnic composition of the population? This process of separating the effects of one set or type of factor from another can be seen as a process of controlling for the effects of such factors.

Controls can be completed using several alternative procedures ranging from very complex statistical procedures to the use of simple rates and ratios. In this section, an introduction is provided to a few general procedures likely to be of

Figure 3.19: Measures of Economic Activity

Crude Labor Force Participation Rate (CLFPR)

$$CLFPR = \frac{LF}{P} \times 100$$

Where: CLFPR =   Crude Labor Force Participation Rate

LF =   Labor force

P =   Total population

General Labor Force Participation Rate (GLFPR)

$$GLFPR = \frac{LF}{P_{15-64}} \times 100$$

Where: GLFPR =   General Labor Force Participation Rate

LF =   Labor force

P_{15-64} =   Population in economically active population 15–64 (or 20–64) years of age

Age-Specific Labor Force Participation Rate (ASLFPR)

$$ASLFPR = \frac{LF_a}{P_a} \times 100$$

Where: ASLFPR =   Age-Specific Labor Force Participation Rate

LF_a =   Labor force in age group a

P_a =   Population in age group a

---

utility in interpreting differences in data items. Procedures for determining the statistical effects of demographic variables and involving relatively complex multivariate modeling techniques (e.g., multiple regression, log-linear, path analysis, and hazard models) are not examined because such procedures are too complex given the purpose of this text. They are extensively described elsewhere (Draper and Smith 1998; Snedecor and Cochran 1989). At the same time, since rates and ratios were examined earlier in this chapter, they will not be revisited here. Rather, we focus on widely used techniques that are relatively simple to apply.

For each of the techniques described, the basic approach and uses are discussed. More complete descriptions of these techniques are available from other sources, and these sources should be consulted for more complex applications of these techniques (see, for example, Das Gupta 1978; 1990; Land and Rogers 1982; Namboodiri and Suchindran 1987; Pollard et al. 1990; Siegel 2002; Kintner 2004; McGehee 2004).

Direct and Indirect Standardization

Standardization is among the most widely used methods to control the effects of demographic variables. This technique *involves comparing two or more populations to determine whether differences in the occurrence of an event or phenomenon are due to differences in population characteristics.* The basic logic behind this technique is that if two or more populations being compared can be standardized relative to the factor or factors believed to be leading to the difference, then the effects of such differences can be determined. If the differences disappear when the factor is standardized, then it can be concluded that it was the populations' differences relative to the standardized factor that led to the differences in the number of occurrences.

Differences in the occurrence of factors between populations can result from two general sets of factors that provide alternative procedures for standardizing demographic data. Such differences may be because the *rate* of occurrence of the phenomenon is different in the two populations or because the *compositions* of the populations are different. The same number of occurrences can be obtained by either a high rate of occurrence in a small population or by a low rate of occurrence in a large population. Two alternative forms of standardization are based on these two forms of differences.

Direct methods standardize two or more populations by comparing the numbers of occurrences obtained in each population by applying the specific rates for each population to the composition of a standard population. This standard population can be any population. However, usually it is the population of a larger area of which the areas to be compared are a part, or areas that are similar to the areas being compared. For example, a state may be used as the standard population to compare counties and a county as the standard to compare cities within it. *Indirect standardization applies a set of specific rates from a standard population to each of the population compositions of the areas to be compared.* As with the population used as the standard in direct standardization, the rates used as the standard rates are generally obtained from a population that is either a parent area for the areas to be compared or is similar to the areas being compared.

Figure 3.20 presents an example of the use of both direct and indirect standardization to examine differences in home sales among two sales territories that had populations with very different age structures. In the first part of this example, age is standardized using the method of direct standardization. Using this form of standardization, rates for each of the areas to be compared are applied to the population of a standard area, in this case the city in which the sales areas are located. In the latter half of Figure 3.20, indirect standardization is demonstrated with the rates for the city being used as a standard that is applied to each area's population by age. The analysis in Figure 3.20 shows that differences in the age structures of the two areas are largely responsible for the differences in the sales observed between the two areas.

Unlike the example in Figure 3.20, in many potential uses of standardization, data are not available on both rates of occurrence for the factors being compared and the detailed age structure of the populations being compared. As a result, both forms of standardization are seldom used simultaneously. Rather, since detailed rates specific to given characteristics are less often available than the age structure of populations, indirect standardization is most likely to be used when data on rates specific to the demographic characteristic to be standardized are not available for the populations being compared. When such rates are available, direct standardization is the technique most likely to be employed.

Standardization is an extremely useful procedure for addressing the question of whether differences between areas are due to specific characteristics. It can be used to control the effects of a single characteristic or to control several characteristics simultaneously. To control multiple variables, the only change in procedure necessary from that noted above is the need to obtain rates for the areas to be compared that are specific to the combination of demographic variables to be controlled (e.g., age, sex, race/ethnicity, and income specific rates if all these factors are to be controlled simultaneously and direct standardization is to be used) or the need to obtain the number of persons (the populations) having each combination of the characteristics to be controlled (e.g., the number of 20–24-year-old Hispanic males earning $50,000 or more per year, if age, sex, ethnicity, and income are the variables to be controlled and indirect standardization is to be employed). Differences in a wide array of demographic factors, such as the number of births, deaths, or migrants, can be examined using standardization, but so can such

Figure 3.20: Direct and Indirect Age Standardization

Purpose: To determine whether apparent differences in the incidence of an occurrence of a phenomenon in two or more populations are due to differences in the age structures of the populations of the areas or to other factors.

Example: To determine if the sales of single-family homes in two different areas of a hypothetical city are due to age structure differences in the populations of the two areas or to other differences.

Given: Two areas, 1 and 2, of a hypothetical city with populations of 36,800 (area 1) and 29,000 (area 2) had sales of 3,570 and 1,932, respectively, in January through May of 2005. You wish to evaluate whether the difference in sales is because the population in area 2 is concentrated in age groups less likely to purchase homes or whether such factors as your advertising, the skills of sales personnel, etc., have created the differences in sales.

Use Direct Standardization in which age-specific rates for the areas to be compared are multiplied by the age structure of a "standard" population.

Given annual age-specific rates of single-family home purchasers in each area and the age structure for the city as a whole used as the standard (note the standard can be any population of interest), the results are:

(continued)

Figure 3.20 *(continued)*

Age	Annual Age-Specific Purchase Rates for Single-Family Homes		"Standard" Population of the City as a Whole by Age	Expected Annual Sales	
	Area 1	Area 2		Area 1	Area 2
20–34	.30	.29	27,100	8,130	7,859
35–54	.19	.23	20,900	3,971	4,807
55–64	.07	.05	8,200	574	410
65 +	.04	.06	9,600	384	576
Total expected number of sales:				13,059	13,652

Difference in sales between two areas = 13,652 - 13,059 = 593

Use Indirect Standardization in which a "standard" set of age-specific rates are applied to the age structures for the areas being compared.

Given a set of "standard" annual age-specific purchase rates and age structures for each of the two comparison areas as follows:

Age	"Standard" Age-Specific Purchase Rates for Single-Family Homes	Population by Age		Expected Annual Sales	
		Area 1	Area 2	Area 1	Area 2
20–34	.29	18,000	9,100	5,220	2,639
35–54	.21	14,800	6,100	3,108	1,281
55–64	.06	2,000	6,200	120	372
65 +	.05	2,000	7,600	100	380
Total expected number of sales:				8,548	4,672

Difference in sales between two areas = 8,548 - 4,672 = 3,876

Conclusion: The differences between the sales in the two areas are primarily because of the concentration of the age structure of the population in Area 1 in younger adult ages with high rates of home purchasing and the concentration of the population in Area 2 in older age groups with lower rates of purchasing. This is shown by the fact that in direct standardization the expected values obtained in the standardization for the two areas are not nearly as different as the actual sales. In like manner, indirect standardization clearly shows age structure effects resulting in proportional patterns similar to the differences actually occurring (when one adjusts for the fact that the standardized sales are for a year but the actual period observed was five months [by dividing 8,548 and 4,672 by 5/12]).

differences as those in sales, public service usage, and the incidence of diseases. Since you often want to eliminate the effects of demographic variables in the search for other determinants, standardization is a very useful technique.

Rate Decomposition

One of the difficulties related to the standardization of rates is the fact that it does not allow you to identify the extent to which the difference in crude rates is a function of the two factors that potentially account for the difference–the differences in population composition and the differences in the specific rates in the populations. Rate decomposition is a technique that allows such differences and the magnitude of such differences to be identified. This technique was introduced by Kitagawa (1955) and has been extensively developed (Das Gupta 1978; 1990; Clogg and Eliason 1988; Liao 1989; Siegel and Swanson 2004) for such uses as identifying the effects of the distribution of age and marital status on the growth of households (Sweet 1984) and the effects of occupational structure and segregation on the index of occupational dissimilarity (Bianchi and Rytina 1986). Rate decomposition has also been used to examine the effects of several demographic characteristics on adolescent fertility (Nathanson and Kim 1989), the effects of selected demographic characteristics on the differential returns to labor among Blacks and Whites (Lichter and Constanzo 1987; Lichter 1989), and the effects of age and education on outmigration rates (Wilson 1988).

Rate decomposition involves decomposing the difference between two crude rates of occurrence. It does so by using one or another form of the weighted average of the compositions and the specific rates of the populations being compared to analyze the sources of the difference. The proofs and computations underlying this procedure are shown in the sources noted above. Although too detailed to be presented here, you should be aware that such procedures can be usefully employed to identify the relative role of individual demographic factors.

Multiple-Decrement Life Tables

Yet another method involves the use of multiple item (multidecrement) life tables. Simple life tables were introduced earlier in this chapter. They allow the discernment of the long-term effects of incremental loss (through death or an equivalent process such as housing demolitions) on a population. In addition to tracing mortality-related effects, life tables also can be used to trace other life-course events that may involve repeated entrances into and exits from a status. Life tables that delineate only the impacts of mortality are referred to as single-decrement life tables. Those showing the impacts of mortality plus one or more additional factors are referred to as multiple-decrement life tables.

Among the most common multiple-decrement life tables are nuptiality tables, tables of school life, and tables of working life that examine marriage, enrollment, and labor force participation patterns, respectively, for a cohort from birth to death. Below, the basic components and uses of these three forms of multiple-decrement life tables are discussed. Although only these forms of multiple-decrement life tables will be discussed here, multiple-decrement life-table methodologies are likely to be applicable to any phenomena in which there is a population with incremental loss (i.e., mortality) over time and for which rates that are at least age-specific can be obtained for the mortality factor and for one or more additional factors of interest.

Figure 3.21 shows the unique values computed for nuptiality, school life, and working life tables. All forms of these tables use the results of the mortality component of a life table and apply the rate for the factor(s) being added to the mortality-related components of the life table. The factors unique to each of these types of multiple-decrement life tables can be seen as columns added to a standard life table. As the information in Figure 3.21 suggests, each of these tables uses a rate, the number of occurrences per 100,000 in the radix of the standard life table, to compute the number of events for the factor (i.e., first marriage, enrollment, or number of persons working). They all contain measures of the number of persons in the state (married, enrolled, employed) and a measure of the number of years at each age that would be spent in that state.

Nuptiality and school life tables have numerous uses for those involved in public- and private-sector planning and other activities. Nuptiality tables are useful for discerning such factors as age at first marriage and the proportion of persons marrying at each age. This information can be used to focus marketing and advertising of products related to marriage. In addition, it is useful in estate and related forms of planning, since such tables can be used to identify the number of years a woman or man is likely to live in a single status at older ages. School life tables can be used for segmenting marketing and advertising and to discern changes in educational patterns over time. For example, knowing how patterns of educational involvement are changing by age and the proportion of persons at different ages involved in education can be used to plan for levels and types of educational services (e.g., to determine the level of need and types of educational services needed for persons in older ages).

Tables of working life are clearly among the most used life table products. They are used to determine how many remaining years people are likely to work at any given age. Such tables are used in legal cases to determine the likely economic loss for a person who is killed or disabled in an accident and in the analysis of workforce replacement issues.

Multiple-decrement life tables are useful for a variety of purposes. Those involved in the analysis of phenomena that have a rate of incremental decline should evaluate the potential use of such techniques in considerable detail (see, for example, Namboodiri and Suchindran 1987).

Figure 3.21: Unique Components of Nuptiality Tables, Tables of School Life, and Tables of Working Life

---

Nuptiality Table

Column n_x	=	Percent of population with first marriages at age x
Column V_x'	=	Number of persons with first marriages occurring at age x
Column N_x'	=	Number of first marriages at age x and all older ages
Column $\% N_x'$	=	Percent marrying at age x and all older ages
Column $\overset{o}{e}_x{}'$	=	Average number of years of single life remaining to persons alive and single at the beginning of age x

School Life Table

Column s_x	=	Percent of population enrolled in school at age x
Column L_{sx}	=	Number living and in the school (enrolled) population at age x
Column l_{sx}	=	Number alive and in school at the beginning of age x
Column T_{sx}	=	Number of years remaining in school at age x and all older ages
Column $\overset{o}{e}_{sx}{}'$	=	Average number of school years remaining to persons alive and enrolled at beginning of age x

Working Life Table

Column w_x	=	Percent of population in the labor force at age x
Column Lw_x^*	=	Number living and in the labor force at age x
Column lw_x^*	=	Number alive and in the labor force at the beginning of age x
Column TW_x^*	=	Number of years remaining in the labor force at age x and all older ages
Column $\overset{o}{e}w_x^*$	=	Average number of years in the labor force remaining to persons alive and in the labor force at the beginning of age x.

Population Estimates and Projections

Data analysts and other users are also likely to encounter population values derived using two other procedures, population estimation and projection. Although often used interchangeably by nondemographers, these two terms refer to separate sets of procedures with two different time referents. Population estimates refer to approximations of the size and potentially other characteristics of a population for periods of time between the last census and the present while population projections are for future periods of time. Estimates are for the past and present while projections are for the future. Estimates are for periods in the past for which population counts could have hypothetically been completed and utilize data from the time periods for which the estimates are made to estimate the size and other characteristics of the population. Projections by contrast must utilize assumptions about future populations or future patterns for the demographic processes to arrive at projected values. Demographers tend to shy away from the term "forecast" to refer to values for the future since the term has a connotation of certainty that they wish to avoid.

Any user employing population estimates and/or projections should use them with full recognition of their limitations and with as complete an understanding as possible of the assumptions on which they are based, because if assumptions are incorrect, estimates or projections based on these assumptions will be in error. In general, analyses of population estimates and projections suggest that some characteristics are related to the size of the error likely to occur. Shryock and Siegel (1980) and Smith et al. (2001) show that the accuracy of estimates and projections tend to follow certain relatively commonsense principles relative to accuracy. They show that estimates and projections tend to be more accurate

1. for geographic areas with larger populations than for those with smaller populations;
2. for total populations than for population subgroups;
3. when they are derived from procedures that directly employ the determinants of population change (i.e., births, deaths, and migration) than when they employ indirect or symptomatic indicators (indicators in which change is seen as indicative either of change in the total population of an area or of change in the demographic processes);
4. for shorter rather than longer periods of time since the last census;
5. for areas in which past trends are more likely to continue than new patterns to emerge;
6. for areas undergoing slow rather than rapid change.

In other words, estimates/projections tend to be more accurate in percentage terms for nations than for states; those for states are likely to be more accurate than those for cities; and those for cities are likely to be more accurate than those for smaller towns, etc. Similarly, accuracy is likely to be greater for estimates and projections of the total population than those for age groups or race groups and particularly combinations of several characteristics (such as age, sex, and race/ethnicity estimates/projections). Because populations change only as a result of births, deaths, or migration, estimates and projections directly employing these tend to have smaller errors. Finally, and quite obviously, estimates or projections made for shorter periods of time since the last census or shorter periods in the future, and for areas that change more slowly and continue patterns from the past, are likely to be more accurate than those for longer periods in rapidly changing areas.

Perhaps the most important principle for users to understand is that making estimates and projections is an uncertain enterprise. No given method is always best. Errors are relative to the setting. In areas with dramatic turnarounds in patterns of population change or dramatic changes in the characteristics of migrants, estimates and projections are likely to have high rates of error and should be used with caution.

One of the most common errors of users of estimates and projections occurs when relatively small numerical differences between alternative estimates for an area are seen as highly significant. For example, when estimates and projections for national populations are compared to subsequent counts error levels are often 1–3 percent, state estimates up to 5 percent in error and estimates for large places as much as 10 percent in error. In fact, errors are so large for very small population areas that the National Academy of Sciences (1980) has suggested that estimates and projections should not be used for areas with populations of less than 1,000. The academy suggests that for areas with such small populations users are as likely to obtain an accurate number if they use the value from the last census as they are if they use the number arrived at by using any estimation or projection method. The authors have often encountered users who deemed a set of estimates for a place of 1 million or more as inaccurate if it were 10,000 different from the final count. City and town officials will often see estimates or projections showing decline as highly inaccurate even if their preferred alternative is only a few hundred different (but the preferred shows some growth rather than decline). Despite such limitations, estimates and projections will continue to be made because of the need to anticipate future events in order to adequately plan for future infrastructure, facility, personnel, and fiscal needs in the public and private sectors. It is thus important here to provide a brief overview of different techniques of population estimation and projection. You should understand that what is being provided is only an introduction to the many methods used in the estimation and projection of populations (for more detail see Murdock and Ellis 1991; Smith et al. 2001).

Methods of Population Estimation
Although there is no single agreed upon categorization of methods for estimating populations, four categories are commonly seen as characterizing the most widely used methods (see Murdock and Ellis 1991). These are:

1. Extrapolation techniques
2. Symptomatic techniques
3. Regression-based techniques
4. Component techniques

Extrapolation techniques are often used, particularly for short time periods past the last census. Such techniques include simply assuming that the numerical increase from past periods (such as the past intercensal period) continues from the census date to the estimate date or that past rates (such as the annual exponential rate of change from the last intercensal period) continue from the census to the estimate date. These values are often quite accurate for short periods past the last census and are often used when there is limited time to complete a set of estimates. They tend to be less accurate and less useful as one gets farther away from the last census.

Symptomatic methods use change in factors that are seen as indicative (symptomatic) of population change to estimate post-census population change. For example, most people live in households and most cities maintain records of housing units added to, and demolished from, their housing stock. By determining how many units have been added to and subtracted from an area from the last census date to the estimate date, and assuming how many (or what percentage of) units are vacant and what the average number of persons per household is, you can arrive at an estimate of the population or population change. If there are errors in the housing unit data or an unanticipated change in vacancy rates or in average household size during the estimation period, then the estimates are likely to be in error. The housing-unit method and related forms of it (made using electric meters, etc.) are commonly used to make small-area estimates. In fact, the housing-unit method is the method used by the Census Bureau to estimate the population of places.

Symptomatic methods tend to use changes in a single symptomatic indicator, or an average of changes in several indicators, to estimate population so that estimates for all alternative symptoms contribute equally to the estimate of population. Regression-based methods use multiple symptoms with the relative weight of each estimator determined by using historical data. The logic is that multiple indicators properly weighted should be more accurate than an estimate based on any single factor or a multiple number of factors that are not properly weighted (that is, those that do not use weights derived from past periods). The most common of these methods is the ratio-correlation method that employs standard regression procedures with ratios of multiple variables to population to determine the population estimate.

Component methods are different from the other methods noted here in that they estimate the components of population change (births, deaths, and net migration). These methods are used to estimate the components of population change rather than to estimate population size directly. These methods generally use birth and death data from the health department together with some indicator to estimate the migration component. When components of change are prepared for particular cohorts of the population, these become cohort-component methods and can be used to provide estimates of such population characteristics as age, sex, race/ethnicity, etc. It is for this reason that such estimation methods are often used. The key assumption in the use of these methods is that made relative to the migration component.

Methods of Population Projection
Most projection methods can be placed in one of the following categories:

1. Extrapolative, curve-fitting, and regression-based techniques
2. Ratio-based techniques
3. Land-use techniques
4. Economic-based techniques
5. Cohort-component techniques

Extrapolative, curve-fitting, and regression-based techniques use past numerical, or rates of growth or patterns of growth, to project future populations. They usually assume that annual or multiyear values, rates, or patterns of growth will continue from the last census to the projection date. For example, extrapolative techniques often take exponential rates for the past intercensal period and assume they continue to the projection date. Regression-based methods often use weights from an historical past period, and linear projections of the future values of symptomatic variables, to project populations for future periods. Curve-fitting techniques simply assume that future population growth will follow a common pattern of growth (such as that of logistic growth) assuming that the beginning census population values are at a given point on the growth curve. All are relatively easy to use, but all also are heavily dependent on a very close similarity between past and projected future patterns.

Ratio-based approaches are best seen as methods for preparing small-area projections if projections are already available for larger areas of which the projection area is a part. These methods are based on projecting how the projection area's share of the larger area will change over the projection period. The assumptions used are often that the projected share will not change, will change as it did in the past, or will change up to some designated share and then not change for the remainder of the projection period. This approach is an often used method for projecting the populations of small areas such as tracts, ZIP Code areas, and other similar areas often used in business analyses. The accuracy of such methods is obviously dependent on the accuracy of the projections for the larger area and on the assumptions made relative to future shares.

Land-use techniques are also used to modify or calibrate growth rates for smaller areas. Although projections of populations for larger areas, such as states and counties, are not substantially limited by land-use patterns, those in smaller areas are often limited by man-induced land-use patterns. Land-use techniques include a variety of methods for projecting when an area has reached its optimum size (usually based on density) or when it is being used for purposes that are likely to make human settlements unlikely (such as a landfill, sewage treatment lagoon, etc.) with the effect that once such limits are reached, growth will be diverted to other similar (i.e., tracts, ZIP Codes) areas.

Economic-based techniques assume that population change is largely a product of economic change; if the number of jobs increases, the number of people will increase. Often, such methods attempt to take advantage of the fact that an elaborate econometric model has been developed for an area and then use some form of population-to-employment ratio to obtain projections of population from projections of employment. This method is limited by the accuracy of the assumptions about the relationship between employment and population change. It is likely to be particularly problematic for areas in which population growth is not directly produced by economic change (e.g., retirement areas).

Cohort-component methods are the most widely used to make population projections. They generally use age (and sometimes age in combination with some other factor, such as sex and race/ethnicity) cohorts together with historical rates of fertility, mortality, and migration for each cohort, and assumptions about future patterns of change in components by cohort to project populations by cohort. They are widely used because they directly employ data on the component processes (births, deaths, and migration) known to change populations and because they provide detailed projections by cohort that are useful for particular types of planning efforts (e.g., markets or services for youth, women, the elderly). They are limited by the accuracy of data for cohorts and their assumptions about future patterns of change in cohorts.

The use of population projections merits even greater care than the use of estimates because there are obviously no data on change in any factor for the projection periods (because they are in the future) as there are for estimation dates. For both, however, it is essential to note that the values they produce are only as accurate as the extent to which population change during the period from the past census date to the estimate or projection date follows the assumed patterns. Estimates and projections are only as accurate as the assumptions on which they are based, and, if the assumptions on which they are based prove to be wrong, the estimated and projected populations will be wrong. This does not mean that they should not be used but rather that they be used only with full knowledge of all their assumptions and limitations. Knowledge of the data, assumptions, and methods used is critical. Whatever method is employed in preparing estimates, or projections, you should not only use them with full awareness of their potential errors but also insist that their producers provide information on how they were prepared and on their key assumptions and limitations. The authors' rule of thumb is that estimates or projections for which the producer will not provide documentation on the data, assumptions, and methods should not be used.

Conclusions

The goal in this chapter has been to provide an overview of some of the basic measures and methods commonly used in applied demographic analyses. Although numerous measures were described, no single discussion can be exhaustive of the possible measures and methods that might be used. You should be aware of the value of gaining familiarity with additional methods and measures for assessing each of the factors discussed in the chapter. It should be evident, however, that the size and distribution of the population and the characteristics of populations can be examined and described in a variety of ways that together provide a relatively complete description of a population. For nearly all types of analyses, such a description is the first step in completing an adequate assessment of the demand and/or market for a public or private good or service and the effects of demographic factors on issues relevant to press accounts. Knowledge of such basic measures and methods is therefore clearly beneficial to analysts, writers, and reporters.

---

1   This chapter is a revised and updated version of Chapter 4 from *Applied Demography: An Introduction to Basic Concepts, Methods, and Data* by Steve H. Murdock and David R. Ellis. Boulder, Colorado: Westview Press, 1991 (No longer in print).

Chapter 4

National Sources of Demographic and Socioeconomic Data

In this chapter we discuss national sources of demographic and socioeconomic data. National sources are those that provide either data for the nation as a whole or data for states, counties, places, or other geographical areas for the entire United States. Such sources offer the advantage of providing data that are comparable across multiple areas, whereas state and local sources (described in Chapter 5) are often limited in use because they provide data that are comparable only within a particular state or substate area.

Demographic Data Sources

Where to begin? The federal government has so many diverse agencies that locating any specific information item can be a daunting task. Most of these agencies have Web sites on which data are available, but even when the correct agency is located, finding the desired data items can be difficult. Similarly, there are many private and nonprofit organizations that provide useful data. We first explore the most widely used sources for specific forms of data and then discuss other more general data sources.

While demographic data are available from numerous sources, the most widely used include:

U.S. Bureau of the Census
National Center for Health Statistics
National Center for Education Statistics
Selected Private and Nonprofit Organizations

These sources are discussed below in terms of the types of data they provide and the means of accessing such data.

U.S. Bureau of the Census

The U.S. Bureau of the Census is the official enumerator for the population of the United States and is the primary source of demographic information. Beyond the population and housing count conducted every 10 years, the Census Bureau conducts a number of ongoing surveys that collect data between the decennial censuses, including the Current Population Survey, Survey of Income and Program Participation, and the American Community Survey. Its Population Division also supports ongoing programs to produce estimates and projections for population, and its Housing and Household Economic Statistics Division produces small area income and poverty estimates. The Census Bureau also collects data for numerous other federal agencies that publish the data under their own agency titles.

Data are provided for both administrative and statistical areas. Administrative areas are those established by law and include units with governing bodies such as states, counties, cities or places, etc. Statistical areas are areas created by government agencies or the Census Bureau for purposes of reporting data in ways that are useful to specific bodies of users. For example, metropolitan areas are sets of counties designated by the U.S. Office of Management and Budget and approximate functioning trade areas with high levels of interaction between counties included within an area. Other statistical areas include blocks, tracts, census divisions, etc. Census areas are often referred to as "hierarchical," meaning that they are arranged so that each type of area builds on the other. The smallest geographic unit is the block; block groups are the next largest areas and include several blocks; census tracts are the next largest units and include several block groups. Data are also included for ZIP Code areas and a variety of other geographical units. You should examine the appendices and technical notes that accompany census products to find the exact definition of each type of area for which data are included in that product.

Data are also provided in numerous formats, including written reports, tables, data files, charts, maps, and reference manuals intended to serve the needs of different types of users. Most census data are now distributed in digital format with the Internet, CDs, and DVDs being the most common mediums.

The decennial censuses are constitutionally required population counts to locate adults by their area of residence in order to apportion seats in the U.S. House of Representatives. The questionnaires from the decennial censuses provide much more than just a raw count of population, however. Data compiled from a "short form" in the census provide a limited amount of information concerning the characteristics of persons in each household, such as their age, sex, race/ethnicity, and relationship to other persons in the household (these items are also referred to as "100 percent" questions since they are asked of respondents in every housing unit). Additional information is collected by distributing a "long form" to a sample of households (an average of one in six households in the nation). This extended questionnaire not only includes the same seven questions contained on the shorter form but also includes detailed questions on additional topics such as education, income, employment, and housing characteristics. All topics included on the 2000 Census short and long forms are either required by federal law or necessary to administer federal programs. Figure 4.1 provides an overview of population and housing items included on the 2000 Census questionnaires.

Data produced from the decennial counts are not released in "raw" form. To protect confidentiality, only aggregate (or summary) information for geographical areas is provided for public use. The smallest geographic level for

Figure 4.1: Subject Content on the 2000 Census Forms

Census Short Form (100% Characteristics):
Questions asked for every person in every housing unit in the United States.

- Name
- Household relationship
- Sex
- Age

- Hispanic or Latino origin
- Race
- Tenure (home owned or rented)

_ _

Census Long Form (Sample Characteristics):
Questions added to the census form for a sample of persons and housing units.

Population Topics

- Marital status
- Place of birth, citizenship, and year of entry
- School enrollment and educational attainment
- Ancestry
- Residence 5 years ago (migration)
- Language spoken at home and ability to speak English
- Veteran status
- Disability
- Grandparents as caregivers

Housing Topics

- Units in structure
- Year structure built
- Number of rooms and number of bedrooms
- Year moved into residence
- Telephone service
- Plumbing and kitchen facilities
- Vehicles available
- Heating fuel
- Farm residence

Economic Characteristics for Persons

- Labor force status
- Place of work and journey to work
- Occupation, industry, and class of worker
- Work status in 1999
- Income in 1999

Financial Characteristics for Housing Units

- Value of home or monthly rent paid
- Utilities, mortgage, taxes, insurance, and fuel costs

which data are available is a census block, with national summary data being the largest geographic level. The primary data files released following each census are redistricting data (Public Law 94-171), Summary Files 1 and 2 derived from the short form questionnaire, and Summary Files 3 and 4 derived from the long form of the questionnaire (in previous decades when data releases were on magnetic tape, Summary Files were called Summary Tape Files or STFs). Summary Files 1 and 3 provide data for the total population and a small set of racial/ethnic groups in the population, while Files 2 and 4 provide data for very detailed categories of racial and ethnic groups. These summary files provide population and housing data in table formats, which can be accessed at various geographic summary levels (such as block groups, tracts, etc.). Only Summary File 1 and the Public Law 94-171 files provide data for census blocks.

Summary files provide data that are already in fixed aggregate categories for specific areas. It is not possible to cross-tabulate individual data items for individual respondents or households from these data. The only decennial census data files that allow data to be obtained for individual households are the Public Use Microdata Sample (PUMS) files, which consist of a small sample of the long form questionnaires for specifically designed areas (called PUMS areas or PUMAs). These areas are designed to be sufficiently large to guard against the identification of an individual household. PUMAs are areas drawn for use with the 5-percent sample of households and contain populations of 100,000 or more. Super-PUMAs, a new geographic entity in the 2000 Census, use a 1-percent sample of households for areas drawn to have a minimum population of 400,000.

The decennial census data are generally regarded as "good" data and are preferred to other sources on population in the United States. This is because of the extensive attempts by the Census Bureau to reach all U.S. households and the relatively high coverage rate of the census (more than 98 percent of all households were included in the census in 2000).

The Census Bureau also conducts a number of surveys to provide data for items not included in the decennial enumeration and that cover periods between censuses. In general, these surveys provide data only for larger geographical areas, but some provide national, state, and some substate level data. Because sampling error (the probability that the results of the survey may be misleading) increases as the size of the sample decreases, the use of such surveys for substate areas should generally be avoided. You should consult the technical appendices for the survey to obtain information on the likely size of the sampling error.

The American Community Survey (ACS) is expected to replace the decennial census long form in 2010. It is an annual survey of more than three million households that will eventually produce annual data for smaller areas (such as census tracts and block groups) for intercensal periods, but data from this survey are only available for areas of 250,000 or more as of the publication date for this work. If adequate funding is obtained and ACS activities stay on schedule, beginning in 2010 this survey will provide annual data for every year for areas with a population of 65,000 or larger and data values based on three and five year averages for areas of smaller size down to, and including, census tracts and block groups.

In addition to the population and housing census conducted each decade, the Census Bureau also produces population estimates for the nation, states, counties, and incorporated places and population projections for the nation and states. These data can be very useful, but estimates and projections for demographic as for other factors (the economy, the weather, etc.) are subject to errors, with the rate of error being greater for areas with smaller populations. They should thus be used with full understanding of their limitations (see Murdock and Ellis 1991 and Smith et al. 2001 for discussions of such limitations).

The 2000 Census became the first census for which the primary means of distributing data was via the Internet. The Census Bureau's 2000 Census Web site has data sets that were previously only distributed in printed reports, computer tapes, diskettes, CDs, or DVDs. Textual data that was previously published and distributed in hard copy are also available on the Internet. Data can be accessed in table format for viewing or can be downloaded for data manipulation. The Census Bureau's Web site also has maps in Adobe Acrobat's PDF format and data files for use in GIS applications. Because access is largely restricted to the Internet, users must have Internet access and must recognize that the items available will change over time.

Finding specific information on the Census Bureau's Web site requires some experience with, and knowledge of, census organizational practices, but efficient access points are provided on the Census Bureau home page [http://www.census.gov/]. The "Subjects A to Z" link is a good starting place if a specific topic is needed. By exploring this subject index, you can access the majority of census-related data for a topic from the decennial census, surveys, estimates, publications, and other sources. The home page for the Census Bureau also has direct links to the most frequently used data (e.g., the most recent census, the Current Population Survey, population estimates). Following a major census or survey collection effort, a page is added to include data files, release dates, publications, and documentation for the products. For example, after the 2000 Census was completed, a link called "Your Gateway to Census 2000" was created to assist people in finding data, maps, documentation, area profiles or rankings, release schedules, raw data sets, and errata as corrections were made. Population data listed on the home page always include a link to "Estimates" and to "Projections," and you will also find a link to the latest press releases with analyses of the estimates or projections.

While the Census Bureau's home page provides ready access to many topics, you should also become familiar with the American FactFinder system, which may be accessed from the Census Bureau home page or by going to the direct URL [http://factfinder.census.gov/]. The American FactFinder is an interactive Web site that allows the user to specify the data items desired for specific types of geographic areas and to obtain them with a few interactive clicks of the mouse. American FactFinder allows a nonprogrammer to gain access to data that previously required an expert user, and the system can be advantageous for expert users who do not wish to download an entire data file just to access a limited amount of information. The FactFinder home page has numerous options for locating profiles, compiled data, and maps quickly, but the direct access to data sets is the most powerful aspect of this site. The American FactFinder's "Data Sets" section is labeled for *expert users*, which means that in order to find the information needed you must know which data file to access (for example, you need to understand that income data from the 2000 Census will not be in Summary Files 1 or 2 but will only be found in Summary Files 3 or 4). Data sets currently available from the American FactFinder include 2000 Census files, a limited selection of 1990 Census files, American Community Survey files, Annual Population Estimates, Economic Censuses, and Annual Economic Survey files.

Obtaining materials from decennial censuses for years before 2000 is more difficult because those censuses did not provide extensive Internet access. Censuses before 1990 were distributed primarily by means of printed materials, so government repository libraries are good sources for the printed and microfiche versions of those demographic data. When you use historical data, it is essential to remember that the census questionnaire has been revised over the years, as have the geographic areas referenced by it. A good example of such changes are data for persons of Hispanic origin that are frequently included in current tables showing data by race and ethnicity. The 1980 Census was the first census in which respondents were asked to self-identify as Hispanic or not Hispanic, so censuses before 1980 will not include this item. Another example is that metropolitan areas are redefined after every census, so values presented for these entities are not necessarily comparable across decades. Some data items are simply not available for earlier periods. Census 2000, for example, was the first census to obtain information about grandparents as caregivers, so you will not find this item for previous years. Additionally, as cities are incorporated, they are added to the list of places for which census data are reported; as a result historical data may not be available for recently incorporated places.

Many of the press releases published between decennial censuses rely on data from the Current Population Survey (CPS), which has been conducted for more than fifty years. The CPS is a monthly survey currently contacting approximately 50,000 households to collect data for the Bureau of Labor Statistics. The survey provides demographic characteristics, including age, sex, race, ethnicity, marital status, and education level, as well as economic and labor force information for the nation and states. CPS is not recommended as a data source for substate geographic areas because the size of its sample for such areas is too small to provide representativeness. The Census Bureau publishes three sets of reports based on CPS data that are all available on the Census Web site, including *P20, Population Characteristics*; *P23, Special Studies*; and *P60, Consumer Income and Poverty*.

The Survey of Income and Program Participation (SIPP) is also a sample survey of households, but this survey collects data from the same households over time, usually 32 months. By tracking both money and in-kind income along with program participation over time, this survey provides insight into change in household assets and well-being, while also providing data on special topics such as child care arrangements, health insurance participation, and public program participation. The Census Bureau publishes SIPP data in reports listed as *P70, Household Economic Studies*, which are available as PDF files on the Census Bureau's Web site.

The Estimates Program produces total population estimates for the nation, states, counties, and incorporated places. Estimates of demographic characteristics of the population, including age, sex, race, and Hispanic origin, are produced for counties, states, and the nation. Population estimates are available on the Census Bureau Web site with a direct link to the estimates home page.

Projections of the population are prepared by the Census Bureau's Population Division for the nation and states. The national projections are currently available by demographic characteristics, including age, sex, race, and Hispanic origin. State-level projections of total population are available, and projections will also be available by age, sex, race, and Hispanic origin in the future. Projections are available on the Internet with a direct link from the Census Bureau's home page.

The Census Bureau, with support from other federal agencies, created the Small Area Income and Poverty Estimates (SAIPE) Program, which produces estimates of median household income and poverty for selected age groups for states and counties and estimates of children in poverty for school districts. These estimates are accessible from the "Subjects A to Z" section of the Census Bureau's Web site by selecting the name of the program. The SAIPE estimates provide the only Census Bureau produced intercensal income estimates for counties.

The Census offers excellent compiled sources that are for sale in published form or on CD or DVD or are free online. These compilations bring together data from several census activities, such as the population and economic censuses, in a single product, with multiple data items being presented for specific geographical units, such as states, metropolitan areas, places, etc. These compilations are particularly useful if you are trying to compare areas in different parts of the nation for such purposes as market screening or industrial location.

The Statistical Abstract is a convenient summary of national data, and it also includes selected tables for state and regional levels. The *Statistical Abstract* is published annually with detailed sections for various social, economic, and political topics from the Census Bureau and other federal data sources; although the volume is reissued each year, not all data will be updated in every new volume. Tables published in the *Abstract* are well documented so that you can review the sources used and the reference periods for data presented.

The Census Bureau also publishes volumes of compiled data for smaller areas, though these data are not updated every year. The *County and City Data Book* (CCDB) is available for sale in published form, on CD or DVD, or free through online access. Fewer data items are provided in the CCDB compared to the *Abstract*, but the CCDB provides data for counties and cities that are frequently not included in the *Abstract*. The CCDB also provides a wealth of data on population, income, health, vital statistics, education, agriculture, labor force, and governmental units. CCDB data are presented first in a listing of all states; then county-level data are provided alphabetically within state; city data for places with populations of 25,000 or more are then provided; and the final set of tables presents limited population and land area data for places with a population of 2,500 or more. Similarly, the *State and Metropolitan Area Data Book* presents data from a variety of sources in tables arranged by geographic levels within states and for individual metropolitan areas.

National Center for Health Statistics
The National Center for Health Statistics (NCHS) is an excellent source of information about health issues and demographic statistics critical for demographers. For example, the Centers for Disease Control and Prevention compiles data from all states on births, deaths, health issues, and health providers and conducts surveys that provide substantial detail on health issues nationwide. These statistics are available through the NCHS. *Health, United States*, which provides a summary of national trends for health related issues, is an annual publication, and current and previous editions are available on the NCHS Web site at [http://www.cdc.gov/nchs/]. The National Health Interview Survey (NHIS) is conducted by the National Center for Health Statistics for the Centers for Disease Control and Prevention through a contractual agreement with the U.S. Bureau of the Census that does the actual collection of these data using interviewers from the twelve regional census offices. The NHIS consists of a number of core questions related to basic health and demographic characteristics for adults and children, supplemented with special topics to address issues related to health concerns. This survey results in data available online and in specialized reports on the condition of the nation's health and specific heath issues for individual population groups. Thus the NCHS can provide data on children's health, elderly concerns, health insurance coverage, and specific problems such as obesity. While much of the data from NCHS are only available at the national level, selected data are also available at the state level. As with many Census Bureau survey data, however, the NCHS national surveys are not intended for use in substate areas.

National Center for Education Statistics
The primary federal source of education statistics is the National Center for Education Statistics (NCES), although the Census Bureau asks education-related questions concerning enrollment and educational attainment in its decennial censuses and provides that data for census geographies. In pre-2000 decades, the Census Bureau also provided demographic data collected during the decennial census at the school district level for all states through the *School District Data Book* (SDDB). The Census 2000 statistics for school districts are available through the School District Demographics System on the National Center for Education

Statistics Web site [http://nces.ed.gov/surveys/sdds/]. This site provides profiles and data snapshots of the demographic characteristics of resident populations within school district boundaries in 2000 for the entire country. Since many school district data users are more interested in their own local data, the profile feature lets users look at a single district as well as to compare that district to any other district in the country. The *Condition of Education* is the NCES annual report that summarizes national trends in education for elementary and secondary schools as well as for postsecondary education.

Other Federal Agencies

There are many federal agencies with additional data that can be useful for special populations. The Department of Defense Web site has links to data on persons in all branches of military service. The Office of Immigration Statistics publishes the *Yearbook of Immigration Statistics* annually to provide information concerning migrants to the United States and data on aliens by various categories of legal status. The Centers for Medicare and Medicaid Services (CMS) has data on persons enrolled in these programs, including an annual data compendium with national and state data, that are available online. The FedStats home page offers options for finding additional information [http://www.fedstats.gov/]. FedStats includes an alphabetical listing of federal agencies as well as a subject index. Another option that provides excellent reference pages for data and statistical sources is the FirstGov Web site [http://firstgov.gov/]. The FirstGov portal to maps is also very useful. Similarly, Geodata.gov provides a one-stop portal for geographic data available at the national, state, and local levels [http://www.geodata.gov/]. Geodata.gov is an excellent source for analysts trying to locate a reference map for a specific area or topic as well as for GIS users searching for sources of data. It provides descriptions and links to geospatial data from other agencies.

Private and Nonprofit Organizations

Additional data are available from commercial businesses and nonprofit organizations. As with federal agencies, a large number of private and nonprofit organizations provide an extensive range of products and services. Private vendors can provide primary data collection services through customized surveys or other means; provide data manipulation and analyses of secondary data; compile directories of selected types of businesses; offer marketing, trade area, or site analyses; conduct community impact assessments; create estimates or projections; map selected characteristics; and provide many other services to customers. These vendors can often provide such services in a more timely manner than public sources, but you should be cautious and only use data for which the sources and methods for data collection are well documented. There are numerous useful sources.

Sources such as the Greenbook [http://www.greenbook.org/] provide listings of companies offering data services and marketing resources with contact information and descriptions of each company. The publication *American Demographics*, which is owned by Advertising Age, tracks consumer trends and offers demographic analyses on a wide variety of current and timely topics. *American Demographics* is readily available to the public at newsstands and articles are searchable on its Web site [http://www.adage.com/section.cms? sectionId=195].

Additional nongovernmental sources of data that can provide very useful data items include nonprofit or privately funded organizations. KIDS COUNT is a project funded by the Annie E. Casey Foundation and compiles annual information on children at the national and state level. It provides an annual *KIDS COUNT Data Book*, with state-level indicators for children, and produces special reports on topics related to children [see http://www.aecf.org/kidscount/]. Whereas some nonprofit sources simply provide data in greater detail than public sources, some provide data on subjects for which it may be inappropriate for the federal government to collect data. The Glenmary Research Center publishes *Religious Congregations and Membership in the United States: 2000* providing data compiled for religious bodies for regions, states, and counties. Some tables, listings, rankings, and major findings from the Glenmary Research Center are available on its Internet site [http://www.glenmary.org/grc/]. Some research institutions release information periodically from ongoing research projects. Some examples, though not an exhaustive list, are the Center for the Study of Religion at Princeton University [http://www.princeton.edu/~csrelig/]; Duke Divinity School's Pulpit and Pew Project [http://www.pulpitandpew.duke.edu/]; Emory University's Candler School of Theology [http://www.candler.emory.edu/]; and the Hartford Institute for Religion Research [http://hirr.hartsem.edu/]. Additional compilations of data on religious groups, as well as data from religious research, may be found in the American Religion Data Archive [http://www.thearda.com/]. Some denominational offices compile demographic and religious data on national, state, metropolitan, and regional levels (e.g., see the Research Center link of the Church of the Nazarene [http://www.nazarene.org/research_center/], the Department for Research and Evaluation of the Evangelical Lutheran Church in America [http://www.elca.org/re/], and the Research Services of the Presbyterian Church (USA) [http://www.pcusa.org/research/]).

Many organizations compile data for specific purposes. Universities are very good sources of data that can be accessed both on the Internet and through their libraries. University libraries and academic departments often offer topical data at the national level. A good demographic example is the Historical Census Browser at the University of Virginia Library [http://fisher.lib.virginia.edu/collections/stats/histcensus/]. This Census Browser allows data users to submit queries for census data from all pre-2000 censuses for states and counties (data are limited to items that have been available for multiple censuses). Current and historical data can also be located through the Inter-University Consortium for Political and Social Research (ICPSR) [http://www.icpsr.umich.edu/].

Socioeconomic Data Sources

Many of the sources of demographic data also collect socioeconomic data. As noted above the Census Bureau collects data on occupation, income, and education in the decennial census, in selected surveys, and in specialized population estimate programs. We will not repeat our description of these programs. Rather here we concentrate on programs not previously discussed and on activities of other organizations that emphasize data of interest to those examining socioeconomic characteristics. Those agencies and organizations include:

- U.S. Bureau of the Census' Economic Census
- U.S. Bureau of Economic Analysis (in the U.S. Department of Commerce)
- U.S. Bureau of Labor Statistics (in the U.S. Department of Labor)
- Internal Revenue Service
- International Trade Administration
- National Agricultural Statistics Service (in the U.S. Department of Agriculture)
- Federal Reserve System
- Other Federal Sources
- Selected Private Data Firms

U.S. Bureau of the Census

The Economic Census is conducted by the U.S. Bureau of the Census once every five years (in years ending in 2 and 7). Prior to 1967, the census was conducted in 1954, 1958, and 1963; and before 1954, components were collected at varying intervals. The purpose of this census is to create an overall view of the nation's economy from the local to the national level, and it is the primary source of data for details about the U.S. economy.

The Economic Census collects data at the establishment level through questionnaires mailed to individual firms (similar to collection of population data from households for the decennial population and housing censuses). During the 2002 Economic Survey, forms were sent to more than 5 million companies, and since these forms are customized to particular industries, there were over 600 versions of the Economic Survey questionnaire. While specific data items vary by industry, indicators typically include number of businesses by type, employees, sales, expenditures, payroll, net income, assets, and data on applicable commodities or services. Through 1996, industry data were classified by the U.S. Standard Industrial Classification (SIC) system. This system was replaced in 1997 by the

North American Industrial Classification System (NAICS) developed by the United States, Canada, and Mexico to provide data comparability across all of North America. Crosswalks between the old SIC codes and the NAICS system are available online, but many new industries have been added and old categories revised in a manner that makes historical comparisons nearly impossible. Economic Census data are employed for a variety of uses. For example, data are used by local governments for economic development planning, by businesses trying to locate new markets, and by policy-makers formulating public policy.

Economic Census data are available for various geographic areas, such as ZIP Codes, places, counties, metropolitan areas, states, and at the national level. The Economic Census Web site [http://www.census.gov/econ/census02/] provides data in a variety of formats, including raw data to download, reports in Adobe Acrobat PDF files, drill-down tables, and information on ordering the latest interactive DVDs. Reports based on these censuses are offered by Industry Series, Geographic Area Series, and Subject Series; historically these reports were published and distributed in volumes by industry, subject, or geographic area, but current reports are available only as PDF files from the Web site. Economic Census data are also available through the Census Bureau's American FactFinder system.

One additional specialized report that merits mention is the *Consolidated Federal Funds Report* (CFFR). Created by the Census Bureau, this report contains data on federal expenditures and obligations at the national, state, county, and place level. The data on expenditures and obligations cover areas such as grants, salaries and wages, procurement contracts, direct payments to individuals, other direct payments, direct loans, guaranteed or insured loans, and insurance. There is an on-line query system on the CFFR Web site [http://www.census.gov/govs/www/cffr.html] that allows users to search for data within each fiscal year by agency, geography, or program.

U.S. Bureau of Economic Analysis

The Bureau of Economic Analysis (BEA) is an agency of the U.S. Department of Commerce and, along with the Census Bureau and STAT USA®/Internet™, is part of the Department's Economics and Statistics Administration. The BEA strives to promote a better understanding of the U.S. economy by providing accurate economic accounts data. The BEA collects source data and disseminates these data and internally produced statistics to the public. The users of BEA data include government and business decision-makers, researchers, and the general public.

The Bureau of Economic Analysis' home page [http:// www.bea.gov/] is organized by links to different U.S. Economic Accounts, including National, Regional, International, and Industry. The National Economic Accounts Web page contains information on gross domestic product (GDP), personal income and outlays, and supplemental estimates. The Regional Accounts Web page includes information on state and local personal income (including quarterly and annual estimates), gross state product, the Regional Input-Output Modeling System (RIMS II), BEA's Regional Fact Sheets (BEARFACTS), and BEA Economic Areas. The Regional Economic Information System (REIS) is a component of Regional Accounts and has historical data that are currently available for the years 1969 to 2003 for geographies ranging from the national to the county levels. Data available from REIS include personal income by major source and earnings by industry, full-time and part-time employment by industry, regional economic profiles, personal current transfer receipts, and farm income and expenses. REIS is one of the few sources on farm/non-farm annual employment data. The International Economic Accounts Web page provides information on balance of payments (international transactions), trade in goods and services, international services, international investment position, direct investment, and supplemental estimates. The Industry Economic Accounts Web page includes information on annual industry accounts (GDP by industry), benchmarked input-output accounts (including capital flows), satellite industry accounts (including travel and tourism as well as transportation), and supplemental estimates.

U.S. Bureau of Labor Statistics

The Bureau of Labor Statistics (BLS) is an agency of the U.S. Department of Labor. The BLS is a fact-finding agency in the field of labor economics and statistics. The BLS home page [http://www.bls.gov/] contains a multitude of links to areas that include information on inflation and consumer spending; wages, earnings, and benefits; productivity; safety and health; international trade; occupations; demographics; other statistical sites; employment and unemployment; industries; and business costs. The home page also contains a search engine and an A-Z index for finding information quickly. The BLS Web site has considerable data available in tabular format and in ready-to-download data files. These data are organized under categories such as employment and unemployment, prices and living conditions, compensation and working conditions, productivity and technology, employment projections, international programs, and regional resources. Geographic levels available from the BLS site range from national to county levels. Customized tables can be created using a query tool that allows data users to select variables for individual counties, Metropolitan Statistical Areas, or states. The BLS publishes the *Monthly Labor Review*, a journal of research and analysis with contributions from experts within the Bureau and selected private professionals. This journal publishes articles on a wide range of research topics, including employment, productivity, prices, wages, industries, and the economy.

Internal Revenue Service

The Internal Revenue Service (IRS) in the U.S. Department of the Treasury produces data on tax statistics from its Statistics on Income (SOI) division and other IRS areas and maintains a Tax Stats Web page [http://www.irs.gov/taxstats/] that contains links to a variety of tax-related statistics. Categories of the U.S. tax system reported here include business tax statistics; individual tax statistics; IRS operations, budget and compliance; statistics on income; and charitable and exempt organization statistics. An example of data available in the individual tax statistics category are the county-to-county migration data. These data, compiled annually since 1984, consist of tax return addresses compared to the IRS Individual Master File System and contain information on different types of income depending on the collection year. While there is a substantial amount of aggregate data available for free access on the IRS Web site, other detailed information must be purchased. Data for other parts of the treasury department can be obtained by accessing its home page at [http://www.ustreas.gov/].

International Trade Administration
The International Trade Administration provides information and assistance to U.S. businesses participating in the international marketplace. The TradeStats Express® Web site [http://tse.export.gov/] is the result of a joint venture among the Office of Trade and Industry Information (OTII) Manufacturing and Services, International Trade Administration, and the U.S. Department of Commerce. This Web site presents national trade and state export data. Topics under the national trade data section include global patterns of U.S. merchandise trade and product profiles of U.S. merchandise trade within selected markets. Topics included in the state export data section consist of global patterns of a state's exports, state-by-state exports to selected markets, and export product profiles for selected markets.

National Agricultural Statistics Service
The National Agricultural Statistics Service (NASS) is an agency under the U.S. Department of Agriculture (USDA). Data collected by NASS are useful in monitoring changes in the agricultural sector and for examining the implementation of farm policy. Perhaps the most widely known product of the NASS is the Census of Agriculture. The Census of Agriculture, like the Economic Census, is conducted once every five years (years ending in 2 and 7) and was conducted by the U.S. Bureau of the Census until 1992 when it became the responsibility of the U.S. Department of Agriculture. The Census of Agriculture remains the only source of uniform agricultural data for counties in the United States. When collecting Census of Agriculture data, NASS uses a list of all known potential agricultural operators and collects data on a variety of topics including information on crops, livestock, number of farms, value of products, expenditures, operators, and hired labor. The Census of Agriculture Web site [http://www.nass.usda.gov/census/] provides the most recent census data options on its home page, with links to previous agriculture censuses conducted by USDA.

The National Agricultural Statistics Service Web site [http://www.usda.gov/nass/] has links to publications, charts and maps, historical data, statistical research, and the Census of Agriculture. The historical data Web page contains data such as the NASS Agricultural Statistical database, Census of Agriculture, pest management, track records, and price reactions. There are links to the data in several formats including text, Adobe Acrobat PDF, and comma-separated values (CSV) for ease of use. The Quick Stats: Agricultural Statistics Database Web page [http://www.nass.usda.gov/QuickStats/] has links that allow easy access to crop, livestock, and other farm data at the U.S., state, and county levels. It also contains links to the Census of Agriculture Volume 1 Geographic Area Series data at geographies ranging from the nation down to the ZIP Code and congressional district tabulation levels.

Federal Reserve System
Founded by Congress in 1913, the Federal Reserve System is the central bank of the United States, with the original purpose of providing the nation with a more stable monetary and financial system. Today, the Federal Reserve System collects and disseminates data on various economic indicators, including money stock and components, aggregate reserves and the monetary base, bank credit at all commercial banks, interest rates and bond yields, and industrial production and capacity utilization. The Federal Reserve System Web site [http://www. federalreserve.gov/] has an Economic Research and Data section with a subsection entitled "Statistics: Releases and Historic Data." This statistics section contains links to principal economic indicators such as consumer credit, factors affecting reserve balances, industrial production and capacity utilization, and money stock measures. There are also links to data on other topics including bank asset quality, bank assets and liabilities, bank structure data, business finance, exchange rates and international data, flow of funds accounts, household finance, industrial activity, interest rates, and money stock and reserve balances. The available data can be accessed in a variety of formats including PDF, ASCII, and CSV.

Other Federal Sources
FedStats provides access to the full range of official statistical data available to the public from the federal government. The FedStats Web page [http:// www.fedstats.gov/] has two major sections: Links to Statistics and Links to Statistical Agencies. You can access official statistics from over 100 federal agencies through this Web site. This Web site has powerful search and data access tools that allow you to easily find the data that you need without having to know which agency produced the data.

Several federally supported databases are offered primarily through subscription and are briefly noted here. The Department of Commerce offers additional compiled data from online subscription services such as STAT USA®/Internet™ and USA Trade® Online. STAT USA®/Internet™ offers current economic indicators for the United States, press releases, and international market research reports, while USA Trade® *Online* provides a database of international commodities and foreign market information. For links to both sites, see [http://home.stat-usa.gov/].

The Economic Development Administration (EDA) in the U.S. Department of Commerce offers the EconData.Net [http://www.econdata.net/] site, which provides links to help researchers locate state and substate socioeconomic data. EconData.Net provides links sorted by subjects under ten broad categories and also provides links by provider grouped by the agency or organization producing the data. In addition to offering links to both public and private sources of data, EconData.Net provides a short description of the types of data available from each source and when possible indicates whether the referenced site charges for some or all data services.

Selected Private Data Firms

There are a number of private research firms that provide socioeconomic data. As with the groups noted above, such data should only be used if complete information is available on how the data are collected and analyzed. Some of the companies providing such data include Dunn & Bradstreet, Hoovers™, InfoUSA®, LexisNexis®, and Economagic.com.

Dunn & Bradstreet [http://www.dnb.com/] has been providing business information for more than 160 years and is widely known for its Million Dollar Databases. The North American Million Dollar Database provides information on 1.6 million U.S. and Canadian businesses. This information includes business codes, number of employees, annual sales, and ownership type. The International Million Dollar Database provides information on over 1.6 million global companies (outside the U.S. and Canada). Data available on this database include business SIC, number of employees, legal status, and annual sales in U.S. dollars.

Hoovers™ [http://www.hoovers.com/] is a subscription-based, online service and a Dunn & Bradstreet company. Hoovers™ provides information on companies, industries, and decision-makers. The data provided includes SIC and NAICS codes for specific industries in its databases.

InfoUSA® [http://www.infousa.com/] is a subscription-based data provider that offers searchable databases for information on businesses and consumer households in the U.S. and Canada. Some of its products include state business directories, a U.S. business directory, American manufacturers, and American big and small businesses. InfoUSA® offers a service called ReferenceUSA℠, which is a database on more than 12 million U.S. businesses, 102 million U.S. residents, 683,000 U.S. health care providers, 1 million Canadian businesses, and 11 million Canadian residents. ReferenceUSA℠ is an Internet-based reference service and is sold only to libraries, educational institutions, and government agencies on a subscription basis [http://www.referenceusa.com/].

LexisNexis® [http://www.lexis-nexis.com/] is a data provider specializing in academic, congressional, environmental, and statistical information. A searchable database of its collection of statistical tables can be found on the LexisNexis® Web site in a section called Statistical Universe [http://web.lexis-nexis.com/statuniv/].

Economagic.com [http://www.economagic.com/] has a substantial amount of data (more than 200,000 data files) collected from many federal agencies and available on one Web site. One unique aspect of the data on this site is that they are in a time series format. Access to the data is free, but a subscription is required to download the data. Much of the data are available at the national level, but the bulk of data on the site are employment data available at state, county, MSA, and place level.

Conclusions

The national data sources discussed in this chapter provide substantial support for anyone interested in the past, current, or future indicators of demographic and socioeconomic change. A majority of the specific sources noted here can be accessed through the Internet. Their Web pages are constantly being modified and you must be prepared to do your own searches to locate these sources as they change Web site addresses or change in other ways. Because population- and socioeconomic-related research are dynamic, new areas of interest will undoubtedly take precedence in the public arena in the coming months and years. Property taxes, education funding, and growing minority markets will likely remain newsworthy but will be joined by new concerns and events we cannot predict. We hope that by providing a wide array of sources we have given you a starting place for your inquiries into the demographic and socioeconomic characteristics of the nation.

Chapter 5

State and Local Data Sources

State and local agencies acquire and develop extensive collections of data for their own purposes and for use by researchers, but these data collections will not necessarily be consistent between states or even within a state. Like federal agencies, many state and substate governmental entities have a history of publishing compiled information in annual reports, fact sheets, bulletins, or other equivalent items. Also, like federal agencies discussed in the previous chapter, state and local agencies are progressively publishing less in favor of making data available on the Internet (see sites in Appendix B). At the state and local levels, data access and sophistication can vary by the size of the agency and the funding level. Typically, government funding requires accountability for money provided to an agency; therefore those that receive better support often provide more information concerning their programs. Data access is generally better for larger state agencies and larger municipalities than for smaller cities and county governments.

From the agency perspective, Internet access saves printing and mailing costs as well as clerical work to maintain mailing lists. Many data users prefer the Internet because it can provide faster access to newly released data, and in some cases data are made available in a convenient variety of formats. The transition from hardcopy data to electronic distribution has been widely discussed within governmental groups as well as user communities. The decrease in paper products, in some cases, has resulted in a decrease in data analyses being made available to the public because some agencies are making more data available but not providing any interpretation of the values. Agency officials are also discussing the lack of continuity and reliable archives of data. If data users receive a publication for a given year and place it on the shelf, they can refer back to that item five years later to verify changes that have occurred over time. With Internet data access, an agency may not keep many years of historical figures available for researchers to utilize on its Web site and some agencies will update older databases as new information becomes available. A user may find it difficult to determine when a data item is "final." Why did an article published two years ago report historic figures that are now not available for confirmation anywhere? The numbers they cited may have been the best available data at the time the story was written but were revised later, and unless the agency is very diligent about cataloging changes, these inconsistencies can be difficult to resolve. Still, state and local agencies can prove to be very useful sources with diverse and detailed information not available from other sources. However, use the information cautiously and make sure it is well documented.

A variety of agencies and data sources are available throughout the United States, and while the discussion in this chapter may not apply to all states or local areas, most governments perform similar functions. By gaining a familiarity with the types of data commonly available, a researcher can better utilize the local sources in any region. This chapter begins with a description of state-level broad-based data access points before proceeding to a discussion of data for local areas.

For demographic data, the State Data Center (SDC) Program sponsored by the Census Bureau, is an excellent resource. The SDC network makes data available to the public though a cooperative network consisting of Census Bureau staff, state agencies, universities, libraries, and other participating state and local entities. These SDCs are the Census Bureau's official local sources for demographic, economic, and social statistics that are produced by the Bureau. SDCs receive copies of all census data released for their state. In past decades, much of the data archived by the Data Centers were in the form of published volumes and computer tapes. The individual states provided computer expertise to utilize census data files before personal computers with large storage and memory capacities and user friendly software were developed. Today, with census data available for download or easy access from the Census Bureau Web site, the State Data Centers still supply access to the demographics for their home state. Most states have SDC Web sites that provide extracts from census files and data formatted to respond to frequently requested information for their own state, counties, cities, and state-defined regions. SDCs may also provide value-added products with analyses of their state's data either free or available on a cost-reimbursable basis. The Census Bureau provides training to State Data Center staff so that network participants can better assist data users who need help finding and utilizing available data. Researchers will find an efficient access point to locate SDC partners in all states on the Census Bureau Web site. State Data Centers are available under "S" in the "Subjects A to Z" section from the Census Bureau's home page. The current URL for the SDCs is [http://www.census.gov/sdc/www/].

Each state has a lead SDC agency with additional network contacts within the home state's SDC network. Also affiliated with the SDC program are Business and Industry Data Centers (BIDC), which offer expertise in data related to local business and economic concerns for states. Both State Data Center programs and Business and Industry Data Center programs have census data for their home state available for local data users, but their additional resources will vary depending on the host agencies within each state. A Data Center housed at a university will offer different resources when compared to other lead agencies located in the Department of Commerce or the Department of Tourism in other states. Likewise, while most Data Centers now have data available on the Internet, the size of the state and resources available to their agency can affect the types of information available. For example, a state with over 100 counties will not necessarily provide the same data items or details as a state with less than 50 counties, and if you do find similar tables or data sets, be prepared to deal with data files or tables of varying size.

Other state partnerships sponsored by the Census Bureau are the Federal State Cooperative Program for Population Estimates (FSCPE), which works with the Population Estimates Branch in preparing subnational population estimates, and the Federal State Cooperative Program for Population Projections (FSCPP), which advises the census on projection issues. FSCPE participants supply state-level records to the Estimates Branch of the Census Bureau to use in the creation of population estimates and review data from the Census Bureau for viability based on local knowledge of their home state. Some FSCPE and FSCPP member states may also produce their own population estimates and projections for their home states and may use different methods than those utilized by the Census Bureau. The FSCPE and FSCPP can be located through the estimates and projections pages on the section of the Census Bureau sites, respectively, or the current URLs are [http://www.census.gov/population/www/coop/fscpe.html] and [http://www.census.gov/population/www/fscpp/fscpp.html] with links to "Contacts" for state partners.

Major State and Local Agencies

The organization of each state government in the United States will vary, but most will have a state access point to help locate agencies within their jurisdiction. Local phone books often provide pages near the front of the volume with easy reference to government offices for their area. Individual state governments often publish a handbook or directory providing information on the jurisdictions within their own state along with contact information. However, since the contacts must be updated regularly a user will often only purchase an annual directory when they use this resource frequently. The Internet provides a better opportunity for states to maintain current records of contacts for their agencies and officials. On the Internet, most state government home pages can be located by modifying the following address with the target state's two character postal abbreviation [http://www.state.(postal abbreviation).us/]; for example Alabama's state government address would be [http://www.state.al.us/]. The home page for each state will have links to other governmental entities within the state. This is often provided in a "Governments" section providing access to state agencies, legislative bodies, and other jurisdictions.

Most agencies will produce some type of annual published report with data, support a Web site with access to data items, and often will provide data in an electronic format even for items that are not on their Web site. Depending on the state and agency, there may be a substantial body of data available for free access, but not all agencies are funded at a level that allows them to provide these services without a charge. The support provided to data users is also variable since some agencies have personnel responsible for handling data user requests and questions while others do not. We have found that most state agencies are helpful to data users and knowledgeable about their data products if you find the right person. Data users do need to keep in mind that staff usually have many other responsibilities in addition to data support.

Although state governments are not all organized in the same manner, they do all require agencies to provide certain functions. Discussion of state agencies must therefore be general in nature as we discuss data sources by topical area, including:

- Health
- Human Services and/or Human Resources
- Education
- Agriculture
- Fiscal and Economic
- Commerce and Business
- Labor Force or Workforce
- Criminal Justice and Public Safety
- Transportation
- Natural Resources
- Recreation and Tourism
- Building and Construction (permits, water, sewer, and related data)

Health Agencies

All states have a department of health, though the official agency title may vary. These agencies provide many important functions within their state including both administrative and regulatory responsibilities. Health departments keep official records on births, deaths, marriages, and divorces. They also collect information on health-related facilities and personnel in health professions and data on various medical conditions. State health departments gather information from local counties and reporting institutions within their state and are responsible for providing these data to the National Center for Health Statistics and the Centers for Disease Control and Prevention on the federal level. Health data are vital to demographers as the births and deaths occurring over time are a critical indicator of population change. Incidences of various diseases and conditions are also available for health researchers as well as data on morbidity by cause. Health departments gather data from hospitals and health care facilities in their state along with information on personnel in health professions that can be useful in evaluating the geographic distribution and level of service for various areas in a state. Since the National Center for Health Statistics collects vital statistics data from all states, it has links available for all state health departments at [http://www.cdc.gov/nchs/about/major/natality/sites.htm].

In addition to vital statistics data, all states also participate in the Behavioral Risk Factor Surveillance System (BRFSS), a federally funded telephone survey conducted at the state level to track health risk factors. The BRFSS provides data on health related behaviors such as weight and related characteristics, smoking, exercise, eating habits, seat belt use, blood pressure, vaccinations, cholesterol, and other factors to gain better knowledge of public health needs. By identifying health priorities within individual states, agencies can better set goals and design measures to deal with those health risk issues most relevant for their home state. State-level contacts and publications for the BRFSS are available from the CDC Web site [http://www.cdc.gov/brfss/stateinfo.htm], and state-level data may be viewed at the following site [http://apps.nccd.cdc.gov/brfss/].

Human Service Agencies
Human services and human resources are interrelated with health concerns and may be considered subcategories within the health department in some states. These agencies are chiefly responsible for providing services to persons with limited resources and monitoring the use of those services. Human service agencies are usually composed of numerous branches or divisions with responsibilities to persons in their state for services related to disabilities, aging, children's health, family protective services, alcohol and drug abuse, rehabilitative services, and mental health. Data available from human service agencies will be specific to the populations they serve and the programs being administered. For example, many states will have a "Department of Aging" within their human service network. A Department of Aging would be expected to provide information on benefits and services to older adults and their families; here you could find data on the elderly, nursing homes and long term care options, as well as financial assistance programs and aggregate data on persons receiving benefits. Certain human service data items for states are collected by federal agencies and can be more easily accessed from their aggregated source. For example the Centers for Medicare and Medicaid Services within the U.S. Department of Health and Human Services have statistics and data related to program participation available for states including some county-level information [http://www.cms.hhs.gov/researchers/statsdata.asp].

Education Agencies
States must fund and monitor the performance of their public school systems as well as public colleges and universities. Therefore, they collect and make available substantial information on students enrolled at various education levels. Data for public elementary and secondary schools typically include demographics for students, data on teachers, faculty, staff, and administrators, results of performance testing, and graduation rates. Public school data collected annually can also provide information on public assistance factors such as economically disadvantaged students participating in school lunch programs and ESL (English as a Second Language). Data for public higher education facilities will also include demographics related to enrolled students, college and university faculty, and

graduation information by types of higher education degrees. Data for community colleges, technical colleges, professional or vocational schools, and private institutions may also be collected by the state agency in charge of higher education, although data for these types of facilities may not be gathered with the same criteria as for senior public institutions. The U.S. Department of Education provides links to the Web sites for all state education agencies at [http://www.ed.gov/about/contacts/state/]. The National Center for Education Statistics collects two primary data sets including elementary and secondary school data from the Common Core of Data (CCD) and higher education data from the Integrated Postsecondary Education Data System (IPEDS). Data for the CCD are collected by the NCES from agencies in charge of elementary and secondary schools in each state. CCD data include demographic information for students and teachers, dropouts, graduation data, and program participation. Data for IPEDs are collected by the NCES from individual institutions of higher education and include demographics for enrolled students, faculty data, completions by type of program, and other data relevant to various types of postsecondary institutions. Both public school and higher education administrative entities can typically be located from the government agency listing of their home state government as well.

Agriculture Agencies

Most state governments also have a Department of Agriculture. This state agency tracks factors in the economic sector relating to agricultural production including farming, ranching, aquaculture, and poultry. State-level programs offer and monitor grants and financial incentives related to agriculture or aid to rural communities. Data available from a state agriculture department will often include crop and livestock production information, sales, expenditures, land in farms, and commodities. Agriculture departments may also be involved in related activities beyond production concerns, such as rural community development or nutrition programs for their state. The type of data available for farms and farmers and ranches and ranchers depends to some extent on the importance of agriculture to the economy within a given state. Agricultural extension services can also offer a wealth of information, and universities with agriculture departments can provide additional local assistance.

Fiscal and Economic Agencies

State-level economic data will usually be distributed among several agencies with specific responsibilities to the state government and resident population. The key to finding state-level economic data is discovering which agency is responsible for these various items in each state's governmental organization. The title given to these state agencies can vary, and certain economic functions may be shared between agencies in some states, so this discussion will focus on the types of data that are normally available at the state level in general. In order to maintain government services, all states collect taxes–income tax, sales tax, property tax, luxury tax, estate tax, or other specific taxes. Most states have a Comptroller of Public Accounts, a State Controller, or a State Treasurer who oversees the office responsible for collecting taxes and reporting on taxes collected. Aggregate information on taxes collected from various sources will often be presented in an annual report for the state and substate tax collection areas. These offices also provide information to state residents concerning local tax laws, which vary greatly between states and can be revised frequently. State controllers will often be involved in their state's budget and audits. Therefore, reports may focus on monies collected and also include the distribution of those funds. State budget data may also be handled by a separate department of finance. Researchers can find states with these data available from several different source agencies.

Commerce and Business Agencies
Most states will also have an agency or agencies concerned with economic development with data concerning their state's economic indicators, business incentives, market resources, or other financial data related to businesses. Commerce departments are good sources for state-level information on trade and market areas, including international trade. State commerce departments often focus on general economic development or promote their state's commercial strengths. Consequently, some offices will offer data on tourism, manufacturing, agriculture, trade, or other specific sectors important to their economic growth.

Labor Force and Workforce Agencies
All states have a labor force or workforce agency that collects and distributes data concerning their working population. Labor force data will often be available quarterly, with values for employed and unemployed workers in the state, wage and salary data, employment by industry, and occupational data. The labor force or workforce office in a state is in charge of unemployment funds, provides assistance to job seekers, helps employers find workers, and may also provide workforce training. While employment offices may be distributed across the state to assist job seekers and process unemployment claims, these local facilities can be immersed in their own workload of assisting the unemployed. Therefore, aggregate data for the labor force are often distributed only through the state office.

States provide certain labor-related information to the federal government, and these data should thus be consistently collected and reported by all states' workforce or labor-related agencies. Occupational Employment Statistics (OES) produce current estimates of occupational staffing patterns by industry along with estimates of wages through a federal/state cooperative survey program. The Local Area Unemployment Statistics (LAUS) is another federal/state cooperative effort that produces estimates of employment and unemployment for states and local areas. The Quarterly Census of Employment and Wages (QCEW) involves state employment security agencies, the Bureau of Labor Statistics (BLS), and the U.S. Department of Labor. The QCEW program compiles data on employment and wages for workers covered by state unemployment insurance and federal unemployment compensation. QCEW files include data on establishments, employment, and wages by industry for counties and MSAs in addition to national and state data. Another state and federal cooperative effort is the Current Employment Survey (CES); this monthly survey collects data by industry and area to compute estimates of current monthly employment, hours, and earnings for the nation, states, and over 250 MSAs. The body of data available from state and federal labor force agencies, including employment, unemployment, hours, earnings, covered employment, and other data related to the labor market, are referred to by the acronym "LMI" (Labor Market Information), and the contract between state employment security agencies and the BLS is called the LMI Cooperative Agreement. Knowledge of the acronyms and agreements discussed above can be very helpful in locating current labor force data from state sources and within federal agencies to which they provide data. More detailed data may be available from state agencies, but researchers may access the Bureau of Labor Statistics Internet site at [http://www.bls.gov/]; state partners for QCEW are provided at [http://www.workforcesecurity.doleta.gov/map.asp].

Criminal Justice Agencies
States may have both a criminal justice agency and a public safety agency, or one agency might be located within the other depending on the state's administrative system. However responsibilities are allocated, every state will have one or more offices maintaining data on law enforcement and public safety issues for their residents. The criminal justice office in most states is responsible for managing state jails, prisons, and correctional facilities, while maintaining records on convicted offenders. It is a data source on aggregate inmate populations, demographics for inmates, and their offense records. Criminal justice agencies may have divisions for adult offenders with separate divisions or agencies for juvenile offenders and youth correctional facilities. Public safety agencies are responsible for issuing drivers licenses and the administration of law enforcement agencies. Crime statistics in general and specific data such as registered sex offenders may be available from either the criminal justice agency or public safety agency depending on the allocation of responsibilities in each state. The Uniform Crime Reporting Program (UCR) has been the responsibility of the Federal Bureau of Investigation (FBI) since 1930. Law enforcement agencies from cities, counties, states, tribes, and the federal government participate, with common guidelines and reporting procedures to provide uniform data for crime reports. Participating state agencies collect crime data from local jurisdictions to provide in report form to the FBI. These state data must comply with the UCR Program standards and definitions for their reported data but can include additional data at the discretion of the state agency. Law

enforcement agencies in states that do not participate in a state-level UCR Program contribute their data directly to the FBI. The *Uniform Crime Reporting Handbook* with details on crime classification and reporting guidelines is available on the FBI Web site [http://www.fbi.gov/ucr/ucr.htm#nibrs] along with publications from the data compiled annually, such as *Crime in the United States, Hate Crime Statistics*, and *Law Enforcement Officers Killed and Assaulted*. In addition to UCR data collected by state law enforcement agencies and the FBI, the National Incident-Based Reporting System (NIBRS) was developed in 1970 to provide greater detail for individual incidents for specific crimes. While participation in the NIBRS is growing, these data are not available from enough law enforcement agencies to contribute to national level reports on crime in the United States at this time.

Transportation Agencies
Transportation agencies at the state level will often have extensive information on highways, since they are responsible for the planning and maintenance of state road systems and, when applicable, other transportation systems such as subways or trains. Public transportation is a major emphasis for these agencies, but they are also concerned with commercial transportation, highway security, and aviation. While transportation agencies may have good data on centerline miles for various highway types, road conditions, and some traffic flow information, these items will not be uniformly available for all areas. Transportation agencies can also become involved with preservation of natural areas and archaeological sites, because most states require site research prior to development of new transportation right-of-ways. Larger cities with dense populations and congested road systems often have their own transportation department that works cooperatively with the state system. Generally the amount of data available for a specific geographic area or type of transportation system is directly related to the density of population and how heavily that transportation system is used. The National Highway Traffic Safety Administration (NHTSA) in the U.S. Department of Transportation collects data relevant to highway safety through its State Data System. In addition to annual data for population and licensed drivers, the states report details for crash data, which include information by types of crashes, vehicles, and people affected. The State Data System coordinating agency for a given state may be the department of transportation, but since the data collected involves accident reports, the state reporting agency may be the state police or state department for highway safety. Not all states participate in the NHTSA State Data System currently, but the program continues to expand. For information on the NHTSA State Data System and available information, see [http://www-nrd.nhtsa.dot.gov/departments/nrd-30/ncsa/ SDS.html]. The Federal Highway Administration (FHWA) within the U.S. Department of Transportation provides links to state transportation Web sites at [http://www.fhwa.dot.gov/webstate.htm]. The FHWA also provides information and

links to Geographic Information System (GIS) transportation applications by state and local sources for all states, see [http://www.gis.fhwa.dot.gov/statepracs.asp].

Natural Resource Agencies
State natural resource departments are as diverse as the various natural environments present across the United States. Preservation of natural environments is the foremost goal of some state natural resource agencies, and they can provide information on the most attractive features their states have to offer including forested areas, beaches, wildlife, prairies, farmland, or mountains. In some states, the primary responsibility of the natural resource agency is maintaining and managing state parks, state forests, and other state-owned lands, while other state administrations will have separate parks and wildlife agencies to manage their natural areas. Conservation and environmental concerns are often delegated to natural resource agencies that then work with local county and city entities to monitor watershed management, soil preservation, forestry conservation, wildlife and endangered species, and preservation of natural waterways. Some, but not all, natural resource agencies house the geographic data related to their state such as land-use maps, aerial photography, water resource data, soil types, topographic maps, and other Geographic Information Systems (GIS) data. In fact, for some states, the best physical data, map repository, and GIS capabilities may be found in the natural resources agency. The National Spatial Data Infrastructure (NSDI) is a federal source providing links to participating state agencies offering geospatial data on the Internet; for a list of state clearinghouse Web sites, see [http://www.geo-one-stop.gov/StateLinks/].

Tourism Agencies
States have differential funding for recreation and tourism agencies, depending on the importance of tourism to the state economy, but most can provide both online and paper copies of promotional information for their state and annual reports on their tourism industry as well. The economic data from tourism agencies can include annual and monthly counts of visitors, expenditures by tourists, geographic origins for visitors, length of stay, tax revenues generated by the tourist industry, marketing and special events promotion costs, and descriptive demographics for persons and families participating in tourist-related activities. Some recreation and tourism agencies serve as their state's natural resource agency, just as some of the resource agencies discussed above have responsibilities for promoting the natural wonders of their state.

Building and Construction Records
Building and construction data may be difficult to locate for substate areas because not all areas require building permits. For areas that do issue building permits, data may be available for residential buildings, commercial buildings, new buildings

versus renovations, and housing completions. Areas with very strict building codes usually require more stringent reporting and therefore collect more data on building construction than those agencies in other areas. The Census Bureau collects building permit data annually from permit reporting places and provides these data online [http://www.census.gov/const/www/permitsindex.html]. Utility data can include electricity, water, gas, sewer, and telephone services and are sometimes a better housing or household indicator than construction records. States with a public utility commission or agency may regulate one or all of these services for customers in their state. Connections for utilities may only be available from very local data sources. For example, a rural electric cooperative may only serve a limited area but could offer very good information concerning the number of connections to residential units, the number of disconnects during the previous year, and also the new connections that were handled during the same period. Most urban areas have reliable contacts within their city government for both building permit data and utility data. Unincorporated areas are less likely to have any building permit information and the utility service providers for these areas are often unpredictable data sources. State-level housing agencies frequently serve as conduits for grants and funding for low income housing or to administer state initiatives assisting families in need rather than collecting comprehensive housing data. Related data for grants, programs, and assistance for housing and persons in need may be obtained from the U.S. Department of Housing and Urban Development (HUD), which maintains links to Web sites with local HUD information at [http://www.hud.gov/local/index.cfm]. While there is not a substantial amount of local area information available on the federal site, local agencies receiving funds and grants usually have reports on people receiving assistance. HUD programs are not restricted to help for first time homebuyers; they also include Emergency Shelter Grants (ESG), assistance for community development, support for affordable housing without discrimination, and aid to persons in need.

Other Sources of State and Local Data

In addition to the state and local data sources discussed above by subject area, researchers have other options available for subnational data. Many states have their own version of the statistical abstract published for the United States. State-level compendium publications can go by different names such as Databook, Fact Book, Almanac, or Statistical Abstract, and they may be published by a state agency or have data from the state compiled by a private company. The subject matter may vary to some extent, but these compendium volumes will typically provide data for the state, counties, metropolitan areas, and cities, including (as available) population data, economic indicators, employment data, historic overviews, recreation and tourism, education data, criminal justice statistics, and state government information.

For historic local data, expect to find little or no information online. While a few local entities may have scanned or entered their older records in electronic formats, there may be no recourse except to do research the "old-way" by digging through paper or microfiche records that may be stored in a state depository library, local library, courthouse, or agency archive.

When conducting research on a local level, do not overlook local experts as resources. For larger towns and metropolitan areas, the city planning office may have already compiled the demographic data you need for its population. Urban areas will often have their own health department, transportation department, utility and public service offices, environmental control office, and economic development agencies. Larger city offices and agencies will even have their own Web site with data and maps available online. Regional data are also available for states through regional councils of governments or economic development organizations. For nonurban areas, the best local source is often the county courthouse; if you are not sure which county office can help with the data needed, the county clerk's office is often the best place to start. Also, if local knowledge is needed or resident opinions and commentary are desired, the State Data Center network includes local participants within states. For demographic data, a state's lead office for the State Data Center program can often provide local or regional contacts who have an understanding of socioeconomic factors relevant to their own communities.

Current researchers should not become too dependent on the Internet as their sole research source. Even if the data being sought are indeed out there on a Web site (somewhere), a substantial amount of time can be expended trying to locate each value needed, and, as noted earlier, older data are often not available in an electronic form. Cultivating sources is essential as they can help you locate data more quickly whether it is on the Internet, is in a local library, or requires a special request to the source agency. Knowledgeable contacts can help to confirm whether the data you are seeking are available. If the item is not available from a reliable source, a good contact can often recommend alternative data choices.

Conclusions

In sum, state and local data sources can be invaluable. Although they show substantial variability in their data holdings across states and local areas, they are often the only sources of some information and often have the most current information for state and local areas. Obtaining knowledge of such sources will often be a very useful investment of your time and energy.

Chapter 6

General Principles of Effective Communication of Demographic and Other Quantitative Data

Demographic and other quantitative data are essential sources of information for many media stories; for such public-sector areas as infrastructure, facility, and personnel planning; and such private-sector activities as site location, market segmentation, and other analyses for product and service markets. Although quantitative data are widely used by the technical staffs in both the private and public sectors and by reporters with a demographic beat, the public and many of those in key decision-making positions in the public and private sectors are not aware of either the extent of such data or its utility for addressing issues of concern. The lack of appreciation and understanding of demographic and other quantitative data is largely due to a failure by those who report such data to adequately demonstrate the data's importance, utility, and relevance. They fail to provide their readers, customers, or clients with an understanding of what the data indicate that is relevant to them and how the data can assist them in understanding what is happening in their community and in making decisions that allow goods and services to be delivered in more efficient and effective ways.

The purpose of this chapter is to provide an overview of a set of principles of data preparation and presentation that can assist those who present data to help others understand and more appropriately utilize data. In providing these principles and examples, we make no claim that they are unique or exhaustive of all those that might be usefully incorporated or applied; they are largely those that the authors have found to be useful in reporting and presenting data to a variety of users for the past 25 years.

General Principles for Policy-Relevant, Data-Based Presentations

Although there is no single set of universal principles or keys to applying them, it is useful to examine any data presentation as involving both preparation and presentation activities and to examine general principles that must be considered within each of these activities, whether data are being presented in verbal, written, or Internet form. These examples are very logical and by no means unique, but too often providers of data ignore basic principles and lose effectiveness in demonstrating the utility of the data. Key principles within each activity area are reviewed below and indications of some of the means by which data can be appropriately presented are provided in Boxes 6.1, 6.2, and 6.3.

Box 6.1: Using Numbers in Reporting and Analysis

Numbers can appear as figures or written out, depending on the size of the number, what it stands for, and how exact it is. The stylistic conventions for number usage vary, so you will find conflicting suggestions from one style guide or dictionary to the next. The following recommendations are based on the current standard practice for most technical and scientific writing.

- Use numerical figures for any number expressing time, measurement, or money.
- Write out numbers if they are below 10. If they are 10 or above, use figures.
- Write out numbers that begin a sentence.
- Rewrite sentences beginning with a very large number.
- Use figures to express approximations that are based on experience, evidence, or both.
- Write out approximations that are obvious exaggerations for effect.
- Use a combination of letters and figures for very large round numbers (1 million or greater).
- Make statistics and numbers in series consistent.
- Use figures for quantities containing both whole numbers and fractions.
- Always use figures for percentages and decimal fractions.
- Always use figures for dates.
- Form the plural of a number expressed as a figure by adding a lowercase "s."
- Use a comma to separate groups of three digits.
- Use a combination of figures and words for numbers when such a combination will keep your writing clear.
- When saying numbers out loud, add the word "and" before the last number. There are one hundred and one opinions about the "correct" way to say numbers out loud.
- Learn what comes after the decimal place. For instance, what is 0.123456? 1 tenth, 2 hundredths, 3 thousandths, 4 ten-thousandths, 5 hundred-thousandths, 6 millionths.

Preparing to Present or Report Data

Principle 1: Know the Audience and What They Need, Want, and Expect
An obvious and widely noted principle in presenting information is to know your audience. The fact that everyone is familiar with this old saying does not mean everyone applies it effectively. This is a particularly important principle for presentations to media users and busy decision-makers. Readers usually have a wide range of news interests, and decision-makers usually have multiple responsibilities. The road to corporate and governmental decision-makers is through their staffs, who generally also have a wide range of areas of responsibility (e.g., for a public decision-maker, transportation, housing, volunteers, etc.), but short-term assignments relative to specific topics (e.g., by next Tuesday their supervisor needs to know whether a local jurisdiction's interest in light rail is widespread or concentrated among a few constituents and whether light rail is really needed in the area). For a reporter, the deadline is often only hours after being informed of the assignment. If you are making a verbal presentation to an audience of decision-makers or their staffs, you may want to contact your liaison with the group and find out who is likely to attend from a given office and their major areas of

responsibilities. You may not be able to present examples that directly address the issues of immediate and long-term concern to all those attending, but the more your examples can reflect the areas of responsibilities of your audience, the more relevant what you say will be. This is simply a specific example of the general premise that people are most interested in data if it addresses something they need to know about.

It is also important to find out as much as you can about such simple things as the home states and towns of audience members, what their occupations are, the basic demographics of the group, etc. For journalists, this amounts to working with your media market analyst to find out the characteristics of the audience for the type of material you are reporting on. Obviously, the amount of time available for getting to know your audience is likely to be limited, but learning as much as you can about your listeners or readers is vital to your effectiveness.

Finally, it is essential to never take your audience for granted or be disappointed by who may attend a presentation. For example, in a policy briefing never show any indication that you are disappointed by the size of the attendance, suggest that you were hoping that a specific person would be there, or indicate other such concerns. The authors recall one instance in which a key legislative staff member who they wanted to introduce to their data program did not attend and disappointment was expressed to a member of that office who did attend. Only later did the authors discover that the person to whom they had expressed disappointment was actually the other person's supervisor and much more important in the decision-making process than the person they wanted to attend. Similarly, always assume in preparing a presentation that the most important people in your agency and the policy-making bodies to which you respond will be attending. Make that assumption a guiding principle in your attitude as you prepare, because you really do not know who will attend. Even if audience members are not in a key role at the time of the presentation, they may occupy such roles in the future. They will remember you through your presentation and through how interested and helpful you were to them.

Similarly, in a media presentation, no assignment is too mundane or unimportant not to merit your best writing or preparation. Every senior journalist was in a junior position at some point, and getting to know your reader, listener, or audience is a mark of a true professional.

Principle 2: Get to Know the Subject Matter as Thoroughly as Possible and Get to Know Those Who Know Much More

We usually seek out "experts" to present or report information on a topic because such persons have the knowledge base necessary to know what is important and not important about a topic, have had the opportunity to think through various aspects of the subject matter, and can answer questions. Clearly, someone who must present information on dozens of data topics cannot be an expert in all of them, but a lack of knowledge is telling and conveys a strong sense that the author or presenter is an inappropriate reporter of this information.

In presenting data-based information, there is simply no substitute for getting to know the subject matter. Knowing the subject matter does not mean that you simply read the script before you make a presentation or read an agency's press release before you prepare an article. Knowing the subject matter means you must spend time beyond that required to address the immediate need of getting to know the sources, strengths, and weaknesses of given types of data. It means you have read background information on the topic (e.g., if you are presenting information from one of the economic censuses, you must have read available materials on the economic census in general). It means you have asked and answered, to your own satisfaction, such questions as,

- Where does this data fit into the total picture of what I am presenting or reporting on?
- What do these data do that no other data set has provided previously (something that is difficult to answer if you do not know what was available before)?
- What are the unique characteristics described in these data?
- What is the time frame of the data set and how does it compare to that in other data sets and that provided in earlier time periods?
- How did I obtain these data and have I actually tried to access them through the means by which I am saying that they can be accessed?

In many ways, what is involved in such preparation comes down to simply read, ask questions, try it out, and read some more. All of us have attended a demonstration of an "easy to use" data product that the presenter could not access or effectively use in his or her presentation, with the effect that any statements about the utility or accessibility of the data product lacked credibility. There is no substitute for knowing your subject matter, and nothing that is more evident and more telling than a presenter, analyst, or reporter who does not know what he or she is talking or writing about.

The other important point is to develop a network of "experts" in demography. This step involves more than contacting your local university, because you want to contact applied demographers who will be more likely to tell you what is significant about a set of data rather than to simply provide additional technical detail, and such persons may or may not be represented in a university faculty. The official representatives of State Data Centers (SDC) and the Federal State Cooperative Programs for Population Estimates (FSCPE) and projections (FSCPP), which operate in a cooperative arrangement with the Census Bureau, are good initial contacts. They can be located by using the Census Bureau's home page and clicking on the "related sites" bar for SDCs and clicking on the "estimates" bar or the "projections" bar under "people" for these programs. Even from these sources you will find substantial variability in the ability to explain data, but you should search for someone who is knowledgeable and careful. The latter characteristic is as important as the former because no demographer is knowledgeable about every demographic subject. The truly valuable demographic experts will tell you what they know about a topic and will tell you what they do not know, and they will tell you when they simply do not know enough to comment. An expert who is always willing to comment on any topic may not really be an expert and could lead you to make some erroneous statements. Developing a network of experts is the key to writing effective news stories under tight deadlines and for reviewing materials prior to their presentation. Cultivating such "expert" networks is well worth the time it may take to do so.

Principle 3: Prepare Your Own Materials and Tailor Them to the Audience
Just as there is no substitute for obtaining knowledge of your audience and subject matter, there is no substitute for preparing at least part of your own materials and tailoring them to your audience. In a verbal presentation, even if a prepared script with PowerPoint slides, overheads, or other information exists, it is essential to prepare your own material for two reasons. First, nothing requires you to learn your material more completely than preparing presentation material. You very quickly learn what you do not know. Secondly, and perhaps even more important is the fact that information for areas familiar to the audience is essential and usually will not be in the prepackaged materials. Too often presenters may miss the mark by trying to be relevant in a way that is counterproductive. This problem is often seen in the work of federal- and state-oriented presenters providing examples from other states or other parts of a state that do not connect with the audience. For example, although it might seem to provide relevance to an audience in Fort Worth to provide data for its near-neighbor city of Dallas, such material may fail to interest the audience and, if the areas are in-state rivals, may be less effective than presenting out-of-state information. For both reasons, make it a policy to prepare at least part of the information yourself and make it applicable to the area where the presentation is being given, but do so with full knowledge (that you have obtained or gleaned from trusted local sources) of the local area.

The general principle is to never use data that you do not fully understand. Although it may be tempting to simply take a chart or graph that an expert provides, be sure you can explain it to others. The authors have often found charts in stories that are pretty but entirely unrelated to the text provided by the reporter.

Principle 4: Be Realistic About What You Are Doing
"Data," "statistics," "demography," "demographic analysis," "statistical analysis," "databases," and similar terms are ones that strike the average reader or listener, as

well as most decision-makers, at best as boring and at worst as means that can be used to support any given position: as the bases for lying with statistics. Many people in an audience are either indifferent to demographic or other secondary data or are hostile to them. Those who are providing such data are often mistrusted or considered as inherently myopic. They are also often seen as taking themselves and their data too seriously. Often, the premise that "these people obviously believe these data are important because they spend all of their time collecting, analyzing, and reporting them" is the underlying assumption of those preparing to hear your presentation or read your report or article. If the presentation is to persons instrumental in funding the continuation of data collection for a marketing, site location, or other analyses, the premise may be that the presenters are simply self-serving salespersons whose views must be cautiously evaluated. What you want to accomplish as the analyst or reporter is to establish that the data are important and useful and that you are knowledgeable about them, but the importance of such data must be established by demonstration, it cannot simply be asserted. Remember, therefore, that before starting a presentation or reporting a story, you are not necessarily anybody's friend, the audience does not necessarily want to hear you or read what you have written, and the audience really is not interested in any excuses about the content or delivery style for your material.

Presenting the Data

No matter how well you prepare, the presentation of the data is the critical step that requires careful execution, and the principles guiding it are of particular importance.

Principle 5: Let the Data Tell the Story and Avoid Providing Your Own Preliminary Evaluations

If data are properly presented, they can clearly convey the heart of a story or conclusion that you wish to convey. This clarity will likely require careful presentation of the data in graphical, textual, or other form, but if you are going to use data, do so only if they make a point. Too often analysts simply present data to make it appear that their conclusions are data based, when in fact they have either been predetermined or are only very generally related to the analysis. Similarly, the authors have had reporters contact them with a story already written for which they want to find corroborating data. Data should lead, not follow an analysis or a story. If the data are sufficiently strong and properly presented, the audience for the report, presentation, or article will have arrived at the conclusion before you note it textually or verbally. If data do not convey information germane to the analysis or story, presenting data is merely fluff. It is better to not use data than to use them inanely.

Although you want your reader or listener to know what the data suggest about an issue, it is usually more effective to first provide relatively descriptive (rather than evaluative) interpretations of the data. By describing what the data indicate in a factual manner in an analysis that carefully tests for contingent factors that might provide alternative explanations for the major finding you wish to convey, you gain credibility, as do your conclusions.

Principle 6: Explain Any Anomalies that Might Exist in the Data and Other Limitations in the Use of the Data

Part of your careful presentation of data must involve a description of the limitations of the data and of your analysis. Data may cover only a part of the population, it may be relatively dated, it may be based on a small sample with a potentially large sampling error, etc. Such limitations should be noted in your report or article. For example, it is unfortunate that although press reports of poll results now commonly include the potential error range for such polls, most reports of census and other demographic data derived from surveys do not include this information even though it is equally relevant. For example, the authors often have reporters call them about substate analyses of Current Population Survey data that would appear to rank one area higher than other areas on some key socioeconomic variable but that have such large sampling errors that the area may actually not rank highly at all if the sampling error is taken into account. If such a story is going to be reported, the potential errors should be noted.

Reporting the error range is perhaps even more important in an analytical report for a business client who will invest substantial resources based on the data provided. If sampling errors are likely to substantially change the conclusions, not indicating them can be costly to your clients and to your reputation as an analyst. Equally important, population estimates and projections should always be provided with a description of the assumptions on which they are based and with a warning regarding the fact that estimates and projections of populations, like those for other factors (e.g., the stock market, the weather), can be in error.

The point here is simply that if there is anything in the data that you are reporting or presenting that you know may lead the data or your interpretation of them to be false or misleading, you have an obligation to disclose it. Those in data provider or analyst positions who fail to do so will over time lose credibility and may do a disservice to their clients, readers, or customers.

Principle 7: Intermix Verbal, Graphical, and Demonstration-Based Materials

Sometimes it is tempting to get all of the descriptive, qualifying, and purely technical items out of the way so that you can really demonstrate the use of data or provide the more interesting materials. You must, of course, ensure that the audience has an understanding of the basic characteristics of the data, but do not leave all of the most interesting or demonstrable items until the end. The reality is that an audience's attention may not stay with you to the end if you do not keep them interested along the way. Whenever possible, mix different types of material with the descriptive information (see Box 6.2). In any case, avoid unnecessary qualifiers or descriptions of data sets without some break that shows the utility of the data. Similarly, mixing verbal or textual with graphical or other data simply makes your report or story more interesting.

Principle 8: Provide Comparisons Using a Context that Is Relevant to the Audience

Many presenters of verbal and written materials, particularly those with statistical or demographic expertise, tend to forget that numerical values in and of themselves do not convey the meaning or importance of a value. In nearly all cases it is important to indicate the importance or significance of a value by indicating how it compares to something else. For example, the population of the State of Texas increased by 3,865,310 or 22.8 percent from 1990 to 2000. Simply stating these values has meaning only for those who know what growth was in other states or the nation. If, on the other hand, you state that: Texas population growth of 3,865,310 was the second largest numerical increase and its 22.8 percent the eighth largest percentage increase among the 50 states; the 3,865,310 value is equivalent to the State of Texas having increased its population in the 1990s by an amount that is roughly equivalent to the sum of the 1990 populations of the City of Houston, the City of Dallas, the City of San Antonio, and the City of Corpus Christi; the increase is greater than the total population of 24 of the 50 states; or that the value means that roughly one-in-nine net additions to the U.S. population occurred in Texas, you have provided a context to which people can relate more completely.

Similarly, if you are discussing differences, it is useful to make them meaningful with comparisons. Using another Texas example, data for the 1990s indicate that roughly 50 percent of the state's growth, about 1.9 million of the nearly 3.9 million increase, was due to natural increase. Texas is among those states with the highest rate and numerical level of natural increase, but that fact will not be known to a general audience. If you note, however, that Texas had the second highest rate of natural increase among the 50 states and the level of natural increase was so extensive that if Texas had had no other growth except natural increase in the 1990s (i.e., it had no net immigration or domestic migration) it would have still been the third fastest growing state (in numerical terms) in the nation, both the significance and the relative importance of the difference between Texas' level of natural increase and that in other parts of the nation become evident.

Principle 9: Maintain a Dedication to Balance in the Presentation and Interpretation of Data

The final principle noted here is again one that is very obvious: objectivity in data analyses and reporting is absolutely essential. This statement may appear so obvious that it does not merit mentioning, but maintaining objectivity can be more difficult in data-based analyses because data must usually be reported in a context. For example, in the nation as a whole, the number of unmarried-partner households increased by 71.8 percent from 1990 to 2000, while married-couple households increased by only 7.5 percent. The first of these values became the basis for countless news stories on gay and lesbian partnerships and was sometimes presented as if such households were threatening the dominance of more "traditional" households. If it had been noted that married-couple households were more than 50 percent of all households in 2000, while unmarried-partner households were less than 3 percent, so that the large percentage increase for unmarried partner households is, in part, a result of a large numerical increase on a small numerical base (a small n, to use statistical terms), the context changes substantially and the relative statistical (not necessarily social or cultural) importance of unmarried-partner households changes dramatically. Similarly, if you are examining data on households and there are data that show both a decrease in the percentage of married-couple households (that some might see as suggesting a weakening of the "traditional family") and data that suggest an increase in the number of children per household (that might suggest to some that there is an increased emphasis on children), be sure to discuss them both. What may be left unsaid or unreported may be at least as important as what is said or reported.

Similarly, it is important to note that different types of information that are presented to provide "both sides' perspectives" may not carry the same weight for different audiences. For example, the fact that the mayor disputes a finding from a statistical agency for his or her city's income level may seem to discredit the quantitative data for the average reader who believes that the mayor knows his or her city better than some government bureaucrat. On the other hand, the mayor's evaluation may be seen as largely irrelevant to the statistically oriented researcher who knows that anecdotal data may be nonrepresentative and sometimes erroneous. In either case, when preparing analytical reports, if quantitative data are available that both support and dispute a finding, data showing both should be presented. If you are doing other forms of reporting, limitations of space and time may appear to make presentation of both bodies of data impossible. Even if space is available, it is clearly tempting to use such space to increase the news appeal by using an anecdotal person or family to "put a human face on the statistics." In such cases, intent should be the guiding factor. If you simply want a statistical lead-in to show that the story about to be presented applies to more than a few persons or households, then the presentation of alternative quantitative data is not as important. If the intent, however, is to suggest that the anecdote to be presented is an indication of an increasing proportion of a population and that it represents an important new trend, then presentation of data that may also question that interpretation is critical. The principle here is, in large part, one that must be left to the integrity of the presenter because no absolute guidance can be provided that applies to all

Box 6.2: Presenting Graphical Information for Different Media Formats

Effective graphic presentation attracts readers, viewers, and users and engages their imagination or senses no matter the media format. Content should drive the presentation form of all graphics. Regardless of format, explanatory graphics should interpret complicated information and provide the reader with a clear understanding of key points and help the reader visualize. In general, think of a graphic like a highway sign. If it goes by too fast, the driver doesn't get a chance to study it. Avoid cramming graphics with too much information. The information has to be easily absorbed. Ask: What is the one thing that I want readers, users, and viewers to understand when they see this graphic? Make sure they get that chance.

Every graphic must have a purpose. Before you design a graphic, make sure you fully understand the story. Treat every element in the graphic as an opportunity to tell a story.
- A graphic designed to convey basic facts should be simple and clear. Conversely, the communicative power of graphics is wasted if they are used to merely dress up a few numbers.
- In most stories involving numbers, change or variance is the story. In mediums that allow it, a graphic designed to illustrate change or a process often benefits from animation.
- Show relationships rather than raw information. For example, instead of listing the numbers of drivers versus mass transit users, create a chart that shows the relationship between the two. And compare rates, not raw numbers alone, whenever possible.
- Where a geographic unit is integral to the story, make sure you show a "locator" on the map—a main city or highway so the readers immediately know what they are looking at.

Below are some guidelines for effective presentations.

For newspapers or magazines:

- Graphics and text stories should complement each other. All information doesn't necessarily have to appear in both the graphic and the story. Explanatory graphics interpret complicated information and help the reader visualize the information. They should organize information in a clear, orderly manner and help the reader to quickly navigate the content.
- Graphics and charts are pictures of data. They should always contain a headline; a line explaining what the information being displayed is if it is not clear by the headline alone; callout boxes to highlight key or important information; and an easy-to-understand line about the source of the information. If accompanied by a text story, graphics should be respectful of the tone of the story.
- Give numbers a context—a visual comparison to help clarify their meaning. Statistics shown out of context can be misleading. Clarify the numbers for the readers. Make sure there is enough data and the correct data for the graphic and no more.
- Don't break the scale just to make charts a convenient size. The wrong scale misrepresents numbers. If there is not enough space to show a bar chart without breaking the scale, use a table chart instead.
- Make sure that text and graphics are understandable when viewed without color. When foreground or background colors are too close to the same hue, they do not provide sufficient contrast when viewed using monochrome displays or by people who may have color deficits.

Box 6.2: Presenting Graphical Information for Different Media Formats *(continued)*

When deciding how to display information, consider what presentation format would be easiest for the reader to understand.

Fever or line charts:
A fever or line chart gives a quick visual representation of rises or falls in numbers or percentages. Use fever charts to display trends in numbers for figures over time. Fever charts should not be used to display unrelated data.

Bar charts:
Use bar charts when comparing item data against each other. For instance, if you are comparing population growth of cities in a region, use a bar or tab chart, not a fever chart.

Pie charts:
Use a pie chart to display information that has parts that add to 100 percent.

Table charts:
Alternating stripes on a tabular chart help readers follow a row of information in a longer list. Use table charts when comparing items with multiple variables in a columnar format.

For the Web:

- In general, limit use of graphics online, particularly "full-page" graphics because the time it takes to load such images can frustrate many of your users. Focus efforts instead on developing databases that users may search to find information they're looking for. Search is the #1 natural advantage of the Internet.
- Include flowcharts and process diagrams and unique captions identifying them. Use screen captures if they can help the user understand how a product works.
- Use hyperlinks to provide supplemental information like definitions of terms and abbreviations, reference information, and background reading. Interactive graphics built in Flash software that contain visual cues to reinforce meaning are particularly effective story-telling devices. Creating Flash graphics is time-consuming.

For television:

- If you put words or numbers on the screen, the viewer will want to read them. Be sure the font is large enough and the graphic stays up long enough to be read. Lead the viewer in and out of the graphic by what you say in your sound track. Make a clear transition from the moving video to the fact-based graphic. "As population figures show ..."
- Graphics that build or disappear help to illustrate change over time. Be sure, however, that you match the rate of growth on the screen to the actual rate of growth. Too much movement can be distracting to viewers and counterproductive. Avoid movement for the sake of movement. Choose a visual element that fits the theme of your story. Instead of a plain bar chart showing that the budget has increased, make each bar from a stack of dollar bills. Or create a money bag, and make it grow to a proportionally larger size.
- If you have words in your graphics, be sure that the track (what you say) matches exactly. Write before the graphic is created, but revise if necessary before tracking so audio and video match.

Box 6.3: Unique Aspects of the Internet

The Web is a unique medium with its own rules and limitations. The key is to design your Web presentation to be scannable, says Web design expert Jakob Nielsen (2005).

In print, a document forms a whole; the user is focused on the entire set of information.

Online, people rarely read Web pages word for word. They scan the page, picking out individual words and sentences. On the Web, it is best to split each document into multiple hyper-linked pages so users can enter a site at any page and move between pages as they choose. In general, Web content should be 50 percent the size of its paper equivalent.

Some other tips:

- Make every page independent and explain its topic without assumptions about the previous page. Provide links to background or explanatory information. The links help users who do not have the necessary knowledge to understand or use the page.
- Use fewer words for an online presentation, and place the most important information at the top. Studies show that users find it difficult to read too much text on screens, and they read about 25 percent more slowly from screens than from paper.
- Write in a "news you can use" style so that users can quickly find the information they want. Earn users' trust by using simple sentence structures and an informal conversational tone. Each paragraph should contain one main idea; use a second paragraph for a second idea, since users tend to scan over a paragraph. And add your byline and a small italicized paragraph at the beginning or end of your work so people know something about your background.
- Useful, clear subheads—not clever ones—are the most effective ways to break chunks of text. To draw attention to important points, highlight key words, and use bullets and numbered lists, but use them sparingly since they slow down the scanning eye.
- Credibility is especially important in the Web world. A few hyperlinks to other sites with clear, supporting explanations for why you're taking users there is helpful and shows readers that you've done some useful work for them.
- Avoid exaggerated claims or overly boastful language; clever or cute headlines, since users scan to pick up contextual meaning; use of metaphors, since quick-reading users might take you literally; and humorous puns that do not work for, or can be misinterpreted by, international users.
- Keep sites updated. Statistics, numbers, and examples all need to be recent or credibility suffers. Remember that more than half of Web users rely on search engines to navigate pages. When users link to a page from a search engine, they should know immediately how the page relates to their query. And they will arrive at your site expecting it to have what they want.

conditions. Nevertheless, always asking yourself whether you have adequately represented information that both supports and fails to support the findings of your analysis, your story line, or your main conclusions must always be a major consideration in completing any data presentation.

Conclusions

Although the extent to which the above principles can be followed will obviously vary with the circumstances, the principles should be of concern to anyone who is preparing a report, story, or presentation. The reporter is obviously limited by space and time and can only adhere to these principles within such constraints. On the other hand, the analyst preparing a report for a business client would do well to carefully and fully adhere to all of them. In either case, you should always be prepared to present all the data that might be interpreted differentially relative to a demographic or social trend and be prepared to defend your interpretation. Similarly, the weaknesses in the data or data that show different trends in different time periods should be reported. If the data do not prove your point, do not make the point either verbally or in writing. It is important to always remember that, in presenting data, overextending the reach of the data or providing only part of the data are the fastest ways to lose credibility.

Chapter 7

Principles for Interpreting Demographic Data and Data-Based Analytical Findings

In the previous chapters, we have discussed how to locate and present data. In this chapter we discuss principles for knowing how to appropriately compare and use demographic data that have been located and interpret the results of data analyses. Too often analysts, as well as the press and other data users, make embarrassing and potentially costly mistakes in the use of demographic and related data. Here we present several basic principles that should help you to reduce the chances of making such errors. At the same time, it is important to note that no set of basic principles can substitute for detailed knowledge of techniques of data evaluation and analyses. The best means of obtaining the knowledge necessary to avoid mistakes is to invest the time it takes to know the strengths and weaknesses of different types of data and how the data can be appropriately and effectively used, compared, and analyzed. The principles noted below are thus meant to be extensive but not exhaustive of factors that you should consider in employing data for analytical or reporting purposes.

Principle 1: Be Sure to Select the Appropriate Items (variables or measures) for the Appropriate Geographic Areas
It is important to ensure that what you want to compare in any data are really represented by the variables selected. For example, a common error among users at large is to confuse family data with household data and compare family income in one area with household income in another. As noted above, families are simply one type of household. Do you want income for all households or only for those who live in households containing two or more related persons (a family)? Do you want to compare data on industries or occupations? Do you want data for Whites alone, Whites in combination with any other racial group, or do you want data on non-Hispanic Whites?

What areas do you want to make comparisons for? Is the most appropriate comparison for cities, or MSAs, or counties, or some other area? There is a tendency for users to want data for the smallest geographical level possible. For example, once they know that data for blocks exist, it is common for users to want data for all census blocks; they soon find out, however, that the number of blocks is very large, making their analysis much more difficult than they anticipated. They also find that the number of data items available for blocks is limited to only those from the short form (100 percent) of the census. In general, the larger the geographical unit, the larger the number of data items available for it, and the smaller the geographical unit, the smaller the number of items available. In selecting an areal unit for data acquisition, data availability and geographical detail must be balanced.

This principle comes down simply to being able to establish exactly what you want to examine for where, but it requires careful consideration if errors are to be avoided. If you have erred in the initial selection of variables or the selection of areas, you are unlikely to end up with the type of data that you need for your analysis.

Principle 2: Check for Comparability (definitional, areal, temporal)
It is also important to check the comparability of items' definitions and their areal and temporal comparability. Checking the definitions is a simple but necessary step, particularly if you are attempting to compare data from different agencies and time periods. For example, a reporter in Texas once made, and reported in print, a startling finding: that per capita income was increasing in an area during a period of dramatic economic decline. The likely error in his data was widely recognized, and the reaction was very negative, ending in the dismissal of the reporter. What he did was to use data on per capita income from the Census Bureau for one time period and compare it to data on per capita income from the Bureau of Economic Analysis for another time period. These two agencies define per capita income to include different sources of income, and therefore the reporter had made an apples and oranges comparison. Even the most sophisticated user can make an error in comparing data on items that change definitions relatively frequently (e.g., the definition of a farm), so ensuring that you have checked the definitions is a basic step in selecting items for comparison.

Checking for temporal comparability is also essential. Data for even quite similar dates may be problematic. For example, when only the state-level data were available from the 2000 Census during December of 2000 and the first few months of 2001, many users wished to use information from the 1990–1999 estimates to estimate the components of growth and simply applied the 1990–1999 proportions of growth due to natural increase and net migration to examine the relative contribution of different sources to 1990–2000 population growth. This is a logical but problematic step because the intercensal estimates of the total population were substantially lower than the 2000 Census counts for many states, and the difference between the expected and actual 2000 count could not be equally due (or proportionately due) to the two major components of natural increase and net migration. In fact, the differences between the population estimates and the census count were due to differences in errors of omission and to errors in estimating immigration during the decade. Without the correct total population to use, estimates of the role of the components were unlikely to be correct. Again, there is no rule that can always be applied about how data for different dates should be compared, but care is needed.

Similarly, areal comparability is often more difficult than anticipated. A marketer from another state was examining change in city populations in Texas and commented after a site visit that he did not see physical evidence of the level of growth that the census values seemed to suggest for a specific Texas city. After some discussion, we realized that the states in which he had conducted most of his previous analyses had limited opportunities for cities to annex adjacent areas, whereas annexation is common in Texas. He did not see the evidence of growth that he expected because the decennial level of growth shown in the census data, which was approximately 45 percent overall, was largely a result of annexation. The geographical area that was the city ten years earlier had had a population increase of only 15 percent. The physical area of the city at the earlier period and that at the later period were simply not the same. Ensuring that the geographical areas you are comparing over time are truly the same areas is critical to any comparison.

It is also essential to realize that the common names for areas and the technical definitions of a type of area can be very different. For example, it is common for the public and governmental officials to refer to rural counties, but technically counties are not either rural or urban. Historically, "urban" referred to places (e.g., towns and cities) with 2,500 or more people, and all other areas were "rural." Even in 2000, "urban" is defined primarily as blocks with 1,000 or more people per square mile (under some circumstances, blocks with 500 or more people can be considered urban). Counties are not rural or urban. Again, it is clear that checking the technical definitions for variables and areal units is absolutely essential.

Principle 3: Check for Sources of Error

There are two sources of error that must always be considered in using data; measurement error and sampling error. The first of these refers to whether a data item actually indicates or measures what you are suggesting that it measures. With many items there is no difficulty in this regard. For example, population size is used to indicate how many people live in an area. On the other hand, density, which is defined as the number of people per square mile, may simply be used as a measure for comparing how people are distributed within two or more areas, but it is also sometimes used to measure crowding. There is no predetermined level of settlement that is considered crowding by all researchers, but because some have come to use given levels of density as indicative of crowding, there is a potential for measurement error because density may not be an appropriate and adequate measure of crowding. Similarly, housing adequacy or quality is sometimes defined as housing units possessing certain characteristics (baths, central heating, etc.), but there are debates about which specific features indicate adequacy and which inadequacy. Using the characteristics of housing units to indicate housing adequacy involves potential measurement errors that must be acknowledged. In general, if you are using a demographic variable to indicate something other than what it is in itself, you need to indicate why you are using it the way you are, provide references to others who are using it the same way, and indicate if there is any disagreement about the usage you are presenting or reporting. The readers can then decide whether they accept your measure as an adequate or appropriate measure of the factor that you suggest it is measuring.

If the data are from a sample survey, you are faced with a second potential source of error. Sampling error is a result of the potential problems resulting from using a sample instead of contacting all population members to measure the value of a given data item in that population. As indicated above, the data provided by the census on characteristics such as income, education, occupation, and other socioeconomic factors come from the long form, which is collected from a sample of households, and so sampling error is clearly important to the users of demographic data. Sampling error refers to results that may not accurately reflect the actual value of a data item in a population because the sample did not accurately reflect (i.e., was not representative of) the households in the population. Any time a sample is used, there is a potential to obtain an unrepresentative sample that may mislead you.

Sampling error can be measured with statistical procedures so that it is possible to identify with what degree of confidence you can estimate that the actual value for the population will be within a certain range of values that includes the sample value. The range of values at a given level of confidence is called a confidence interval. Most census and other survey data will contain information on the confidence intervals for different sample sizes from a given population. Usually 95 or 90 percent confidence levels are employed, indicating that there is a 95 or 90 percent probability that the actual population value is contained within a given range of values (is within the range of values covered by the confidence interval). This range of values (the confidence interval of values) will be wider the more certain you want to be that the actual population value is included in the interval (i.e., it will be wider for a 95 percent confidence interval than a 90 percent, and a 90 percent interval wider than an 80 percent interval). The size of the sample (as a proportion of the total population) affects sample accuracy. In general, the larger the sample as a proportion of the population, the smaller the confidence interval and the lower the sampling error, while the smaller the sample, the larger the potential sampling error. For example, if mean income levels are being compared, before noting that the areas are quite different in terms of income, be sure to check the sampling error and the related confidence interval, which are commonly provided in Census publications. Thus, if the average income levels in two areas vary from one another by $2,000 dollars, but the confidence interval for income for one of the areas is inclusive of the value for the other area, then the two areas may have identical income levels that are masked by sampling error. Particularly in private-sector uses where markets may be sensitive to income differences, the failure to take such errors into account can be very costly.

For areas with very small populations, confidence intervals may be very large, sampling error rates quite high, and reported sample values of questionable utility. For example, Loving County, Texas, was the only county in the United States in the 2000 Census to be reported as having zero households in poverty. With only 67 residents (making it the smallest county in the nation) and 31 households, however, a sample from the county is subject to substantial sampling error. Loving County did have households in poverty, but they were simply not included in the sample of households contacted by the Census. Although Loving County is an extreme example because no other county is as small, it is important to recognize that such cautions are also applicable to block groups, tracts, and other areas with small population sizes.

Assistance in finding sampling errors is readily available in census data reports and other survey reports. All census reports, whether they are in electronic or printed form, will have an appendix that shows the sampling error for each area, the likely sampling errors of geographic units of different sizes, and/or a simple formula for computing such errors.

Principle 4: Assess the Demographic and Socioeconomic Context
Ensuring that the differences in the demographic and socioeconomic context of areas are recognized in comparisons may require more experience than the other factors described above. For example, on numerous occasions we have seen both media and other reports comparing areas on specific characteristics and providing speculations about the social and other factors causing such differences. These comparisons sometimes display a naivete about the effects of differences in other demographic characteristics that likely explain the differences rather than the highlighted characteristics or processes suggested by the author. In one instance, an area with rapid population growth had also shown a rapid increase in the number of married-couple families. This area was highlighted in a press profile that included several anecdotal interviews with people who noted the emphasis placed on children by residents of the area. The numerical increase in married-couple households in this area was used as an indication of an increasing pro-child societal emphasis. Whether such an emphasis did or did not exist, the reality was that the area in question had experienced more rapid population growth due to a substantial increase in its Hispanic population. Because Hispanic households include a higher proportion of married-couple families than non-Hispanic White households, much of the differences in married-couple households observed between this area and others was because of the larger proportion of its growth that was due to Hispanic populations. If the differential effects of Hispanic households were removed, there was little evidence that the area had a disproportionate increase in married-couple

families. The pattern noted was due to demographic compositional differences rather than unique societal patterns.

An even more serious example of comparisons that ignore demographic determinants was an account in the press noting that paroled child molesters in one city tended to live in areas with more children. Further analysis suggested, however, that there were more children in areas with lower housing values and rents, and more paroled child molesters lived in areas with lower housing values and rents. A critic of the press account pointed out that it was important to note this likely common determinant because in some areas with higher housing values and rents, but equally high numbers of children, there were few paroled child molesters in residence.

The lesson here is that if you are trying to point out specific patterns, be careful to compare similar areas so that you are not implying causation to differences that may be a result of a factor common to both differences that was not included in your analysis. You can obviously only check for some of these factors for any given data use, but checking for some of the most obvious can allow you to avoid embarrassment.

Principle 5: Compare Results Against Expected Trends

One of the most important characteristics in analyzing data to determine its utility is that of skepticism toward your own findings. In analyzing data, the authors have found it useful once they have arrived at a conclusion from their data to assume that they are wrong in their interpretation and to make the data prove them correct. This requires that you keep searching all the means by which you might be wrong, ways in which the data may have been miscollected, or incorrect or mislabeled data items used, until you become comfortable with the findings. If you assume you are right, you are likely to be complacent and prematurely stop examining the data and your findings.

We recommend the use of several comparisons to assess your data and the findings from it. Ask yourself the following questions:

- Is the value or finding for the area examined consistent with that for the larger areas of which it is a part, or does it present a somewhat unique data item or finding?
- Is the finding consistent with patterns for other similar areas (suburbs, central cities, rural areas, regions such as the Great Plains or Deep South, border counties, etc.)?
- If the finding for your area of interest is unique, is it because the characteristics of its population are unique or because of other factors?
- Is a finding for your area of interest significant relative to the nation, the state, or other areas in proximity to the one you have examined; or relative to expected year-to-year or time-to-time fluctuations?

- Is the change (trend) leading in directions evident in other similar areas and for similar items or characteristics (e.g., is the pattern similar to that for other families, for the same ethnic group in other areas)?

In general, component areas tend to show similar patterns, such as similar patterns of slow or rapid growth, similar patterns of ethnic diversification, etc. If your area of interest is showing patterns different from the area of which it is a part, be sure that your findings are correct, that you really do have a unique area.

Similarly, there is surprising similarity in the patterns for different types of areas, such as suburban areas, central cities, and rural areas. Suburbs tend to be faster growing but less diverse and have disproportionate numbers of young adults with children, while central cities tend to be slower growing, more diverse, and to have older, more adult-dominated populations. Rural areas tend to have slow growth, more limited diversity, and older populations. Some regions such as the Great Plains have had quite homogeneous populations and decades of slow growth, while many areas in the South and West have had substantial growth and diversity. If the area you are examining departs from the patterns for other areas of its type and region, again be sure that this departure is real and not based on errors in data collection or interpretation.

If the area you are examining has unique patterns, try to explain that uniqueness. Are its patterns different because the characteristics of the population are different, or are the differences due to other factors? For example, populations often appear to have abnormally high crude birth or death rates or rates of crime, all of which are influenced by the age composition of the population. Populations with large numbers of young adults tend to have higher birth rates, areas with older populations tend to have higher death rates, and populations with high percentages of their populations in those ages associated with criminal activity (i.e., the late teens and early 20s) are likely to have higher crime rates. Before you conclude, for example, that a suburb's birth rates are particularly high because of profamily values, concentration in given ethnic or religious groups, or other such reasons (and draw other conclusions on other topics based on nondemographic factors), be sure that the answer is not simply that the population in that suburb has characteristics that are different from those in comparison areas. An example of compositional change that has often been attributed almost totally to nondemographic factors is the growth of home ownership in the 1990s. Many newspapers and other media sources have presented stories interviewing loan experts, economists, family experts, and others to explain the trend. Among the causes often noted have been Americans' desire to be owners, the role that home ownership plays in obtaining the American Dream, and similar factors. Such factors may have played an important role and it is clear that had interest rates been abnormally high ownership rates may not have increased, but there was a very important demographic reason as well.

Rates of home ownership by age have remained relatively constant over time, with the peak rates occurring in the middle ages of the life cycle. The 1990s witnessed an explosion in the growth of middle-aged populations fostered by the baby-boom generation entering middle ages. This explanation has received very little attention in the popular media but is a good example of why it is important to determine whether a change is due to differences in the characteristics of the populations being compared (in this case, the change in the U.S. population's age structure in the 1990s) before attributing the change to other factors.

It is important to note whether the change observed is really that dramatic relative to other areas that are similar in form and location. For example, in a rapidly growing suburban county with growth rates of 2 to 3 percent per year, highlighting such growth in one of the cities as a reflection of its superior economic development efforts might be misleading. The trends in subareas are sometimes carried along by the areas of which they are a part, so growth levels cannot be examined in a vacuum but should be evaluated only in comparison to other similar areas in similar locations.

It is also important to discern whether a change is substantively significant. If you are examining change in rates of population growth, increases in the number of households, increases in home ownership, and other such factors, determine whether the difference is substantively significant and indicative of a long-term change. For example, births for even relatively large areas may fluctuate from year to year. As a result, demographers tend to use an average number of births for several years in projecting long-term fertility patterns. The authors recall a reporter from a moderate-sized city who decided that an increase in births was so high that it was indicative of trends in the area's emphasis on children, with the increased importance of children obviously fueling the increase in the number of births. Although informed that this change in the number of births could be a chance fluctuation because there were other years in which the number of births in the area had increased or decreased substantially, the reporter wrote the story. The apparent emphasis on children he reported must have dissipated over the next year, however, because the number of births declined. Similar errors are possible for numerous factors.

Yet another important means of evaluating the reasonableness of an observed change is to examine a variable relative to expected long-term patterns for the data item, for similar areas, and for the state and nation as a whole. Is the pattern of ethnic change suggesting that an area is becoming more homogeneous when other areas are becoming more diverse? Is the population for the area becoming younger when most areas' populations are becoming older? If the trends in your area of interest are contrary to those in most similar areas, be sure that your data and your analyses are correct.

Getting to know the basic trends for the nation, the state, and local areas is extremely valuable in your evaluation of trends in an area. Examine summary reports for the nation from the Census Bureau, reports from your state demographer's office about the state, and reports by local demographers and planners about the local area. With this base of knowledge, you will be much better prepared to evaluate the reasonableness of your findings.

Some trends are so pervasive that they should always be considered as you evaluate the data you have obtained:

1. In the United States, areas in the West and South have been growing faster than areas in the Northeast and Midwest.
2. Suburban growth has been greater than central city growth and is fueled more by domestic migration, while rural areas have shown growth that is generally the slowest of all areas, is occasionally faster than growth in central cities, but is rarely faster than that in suburbs.
3. Because of the aging of the baby-boom generation, populations in the United States are growing older (in median or mean age terms) and are expected to continue to do so for several decades.
4. There are more males than females at birth, but males die at higher rates at all ages, and so there are substantially more females than males at older ages.
5. Minority groups, particularly Hispanics, are showing higher growth rates and generally have younger populations than non-Hispanic White or African American populations.
6. The proportion of all households that are nonfamily households has been increasing, and among family households, single-parent families have shown the highest rates of growth.
7. Educational attainment is generally increasing, but there are large differentials between educational attainment rates for non-Hispanic Whites and Asians and those rates for African Americans and Hispanics.
8. The highest rates of growth in employment have been in the service industries, with slower growth in other industries and decline in the percentage of employees in many extractive industries such as agriculture.

If your analysis suggests trends that are different from these, you may not be wrong, but you would do well to recheck your values, check with a knowledgeable expert about what you have found, etc. Deviations from such patterns are simply warning signs that may indicate an error, and the cautious analyst uses them to identify potential problems and reexamines his or her analysis to ensure that the findings are correct.

Conclusions

The principles noted above will not guarantee that you will avoid mistakes in interpreting data, but they should reduce your chances of doing so. Overall, they should indicate how essential it is to use caution in interpreting demographic and other data and how essential comparisons to other areas and review of technical appendices can be in avoiding errors. For readers who find the list of tasks suggested by these principles to be somewhat daunting, it should be noted that the best teacher of all in this, as in many things, is experience. As you use demographic data, you will come to know their unique advantages and disadvantages in completing your analysis or telling your story. Hopefully, the principles provided here will help shorten the learning curve for accurately and appropriately interpreting, and for effectively using, demographic data.

Chapter 8

Examples of the Use and
Misuse of Demographic Data

In the preceding chapters we have provided an overview of the sources of demographic data, methods of analyses, and principles for using and communicating the results of demographic analyses. In this chapter, we provide examples of the use of demographic data for different areas of analysis and reporting. Examples are provided from the media, business, and government. For each example, we describe the context in which the particular example occurred, how data were located, presented, and used, and the results of the analysis, and we provide some lessons from the examples that demonstrate the utility of the principles noted in Chapters 6 and 7. Since we provide examples of both inappropriate and appropriate uses of demographic data, we do not always provide the actual names of the companies, governments, media outlets, or individuals involved. The examples are of real uses by real users, however, and hopefully help demonstrate how to appropriately and effectively use, and how not to use, demographic data for analyses of events and conditions of importance to the media and the private and public sectors.

Media Uses of Demographic Data

In 1996, Texas State Demographer Steve Murdock (then at Texas A&M University and now at The University of Texas at San Antonio) and his colleagues at the Texas State Data Center prepared a report for the state Legislature documenting troubling socioeconomic trends. At the time, it was the most comprehensive study ever on the implications of the state's long-term demographic trends, which the team had spent three years discerning from the U.S. Census and other official measurements.

The data were first presented during the Texas State Data Center's annual meeting in Austin. The conference, which drew over seventy-five demographers from across the state, featured, among many programs, an overview of the data center's work plan.

At the conference, Dr. Murdock previewed the data on dozens of slides using presentation software. The reporter (who is the second author of this book) took copious notes on the presentation—not for a daily newspaper report (the data were far too complicated to rush into the daily newspaper), but for what looked more promising as a story for the Sunday newspaper. At the conference, the reporter made arrangements to visit Dr. Murdock to review his findings in detail. It took a full day to walk through the data—two volumes, each nearly two inches thick—and grasp not only their overall significance, but also their nuances.

The reporter used the data and the knowledge digested from the review to prepare a large Sunday newspaper story—text that started on the front page of the newspaper and ran on two more full newspaper pages inside. The text was accompanied by a dozen graphics illustrating key information—"factoids"— from the data.

On July 28, 1996, *The Dallas Morning News*, a newspaper with a circulation of nearly 900,000 (then), carried a front page story on the report with phrases such as the following:

> Texans reaching adulthood in 1996 may be the state's first generation who really can say their best days are behind them. For if demography offers a clue about destiny, Texas in the year 2030 could be a sobering place if worrisome socioeconomic trends aren't addressed, according to a new study conducted for the Texas Legislature.

> Cities swelling with new millions living in poverty. Stretched welfare rolls overwhelming taxpayers' tolerance. Shrinking numbers of highly educated, well-paid employees. Expanding numbers of minimally skilled workers. If current population trends go unchanged, these conditions were likely to be the future Texans faced. Altering that possible path is Texas' foremost challenge.

> If we don't want a society that is less educated, poorer and increasingly violent, we're going to have to identify things to invest in the future of Texas right now. We must recognize that these investments will be larger and more long-term than we would prefer them to be. But it will be less than the cost of not investing.

This report was later published as a book, *The Texas Challenge: Population Change and the Future of Texas* (1997). It became one of the most influential state reports in Texas history.

Teel Bivins, the U.S. Ambassador to Sweden who served in the Texas State Senate from 1989 to 2004 as a Republican from Amarillo, said in a preface to an updated version of the report: "I know of no work that offers a clearer vision of what is at stake for our state than the book you currently hold in your hands" (Murdock et al. 2003: xxxiv).

The turning point for Texas, according to Dr. Murdock, will be the socioeconomic fortune of its minority population—the fastest growing group and historically the most disadvantaged. As Texas minorities collectively become the majority—a milestone reached in 2004—their growing numbers will ripple through virtually every facet of life. For a variety of reasons—discrimination, poverty, lack of opportunity—the minority population in Texas has not reached the level of income and education of the state's non-Hispanic White population.

Unless those gaps are narrowed substantially before 2030, Texans as a whole will earn less, be less educated, and occupy lower skilled jobs than they do today. In other words, Texas would be headed in a direction that is opposite that which experts say is required to remain competitive in a global marketplace: toward a highly educated workforce trained for good-paying high-tech jobs.

Former Texas Lieutenant Governor William P. Hobby Jr., a Democrat from Houston, said of the report now updated with Census 2000 figures and republished in 2003 as *The New Texas Challenge: Population Change and the Future of Texas*,

> We have been given a wakeup call here. . . . The policy implications of the numbers are clear. Do we face up to them, or do we once again lapse into the economic and educational mediocrity that characterized Texas fifty years ago. The information in this book projects the future of Texas—unless we wise up (Murdock et al. 2003:xxxiv-xli).

Fast forward to 2004. It is a Wednesday in mid-September and the packed Austin, Texas, courtroom awaits a ruling by Texas State District Judge John Dietz on the constitutionality of the state's school finance system. The ruling follows six weeks of testimony in a lawsuit brought by 300 school districts that objected to the state's "share-the-wealth" finance method. Even rich school districts were part of the lawsuit because they object to sending tax money collected within their districts to other districts.

The judge's ruling was that the state of Texas must provide more money for Texas schools by October 2005 or the system must shut down. A key factor in his decision: a 500-page report by state demographer Steve Murdock, et al., which was introduced at the trial. Judge Dietz cited Murdock's research that showed a significant disparity between rich and poor with regard to student achievement, which the judge said would get worse if not addressed. If the education gap persists on into the year 2040, the judge said,

> Texas in 2040 will have a population that is larger, poorer, less educated and more needy than today. Who in Texas would choose this as our future? The answer is no one. Not a single

Texan, from Brownsville to Dalhart or El Paso to Beaumont, would pick that as a future for Texas. . . . The key to changing our future is to close the gap in academic achievement between the haves and the have-nots. The state demographer projects that if we could close the gap in educational achievement just half way by 2020, then Texas would be wealthier than today in real dollars, spend more money for our economy, pay more taxes for our government.

What lessons can be gleaned from this case? Listen carefully when data are presented. Listen not only for overall significance, but for nuances. When writing about data related to demography, do not rush. Review data carefully with its "author." Do not assume that a dispassionate reading of data will provide needed understanding of the material. To confirm understanding, repeat major findings and define their limitations with the author.

Consider breaking important facts into small graphical elements, such as pie, table, and bar charts. Complicated material divided into bite-size pieces greatly improves reader comprehension. Too many graphics, on the other hand, regardless of their individual value, can overwhelm the reader.

Review the length of written text. Make certain that paragraphs are not overloaded with numbers. Too many numbers weigh down text. In retrospect, the story could have been reduced in size by one quarter. Careful and concise writing is essential, and learning how to write about numerical information is a skill that will be invaluable (see Box 8.1 for tips on writing about numerical information).

Finally, learn to recognize important work and give it its due. Important data will take on more significance over time. Only by keeping current on demographic and policy trends can you recognize such work. The need for constant study and reading is indispensable to the good reporter.

Business Uses and Misuses of Demographic Data

Businesses use demographic data in a myriad of ways, and excellent examples are available in Kintner et al. (1995), Siegel (2002), and a wide variety of business journals in areas such as marketing and management. Here we present examples related to three business uses: site selection for a convenience store, determination of the market for a nursing home in a rural area, and an assessment of EEO compliance in corporate hiring. In these examples, we identify excellent and less than excellent uses of demographic data and analyses.

A Mis-sited Site or a Misunderstood Business?
A small in-state chain of convenience stores had decided to expand into a market in a moderate-sized urban location that involved two sister cities of approximately

equal size. Although these two cities together had only about 100,000 people, they were substantially larger than the communities in which the chain had been operating. In fact, the chain owned and operated stores largely in rural areas in East Texas where the chain's stores were often the only major source of grocery and drug products within 15 miles or more. Its customer profile consisted largely of lower-middle class patrons working in extractive industries, such as agriculture, mining, and timber processing.

The owners contracted with the authors to complete a site selection analysis within the sister-city community in which the authors lived. The owners indicated that there were sites at three alternative street corners available in the two cities and asked that the authors make a recommendation relative to the three sites. Two of the three sites were in the older of the two cities that was a traditional southern trade center while the third was in the other community that was a college town in which more than 85 percent of the population was composed of students, faculty, and others who worked in businesses directly dependent on the university.

The authors took a very academic approach to the analysis. They searched the business literature on store location analysis techniques and obtained trade data about the profile of the average convenience store customer. They obtained GIS-based maps of the three site areas, met with local municipal and highway department planners to obtain information on highway traffic flows and commuting times, and obtained data on actual and projected populations and households for the area. Data on the current characteristics of the population were taken from the most recent census, with data being used at the tract level because of evidence suggesting that users of a convenience store tend to be drawn from areas in close proximity to the store and because of the desire to have data on income as well as other socioeconomic characteristics, which were not available at the block level. Data from Census SF1 and SF3 formed the major data sources. Population projections were obtained from the State Demographer's office and were for the county level. Since more than 90 percent of the population in the county was in the two cities, these projections were deemed to be an appropriate base for examining future trends. The authors used GIS-based methods to establish the number of people in tracts at various distances from the potential sites at the two most recent censuses so that the trend in the share of the total county population in each tract could be obtained and projected forward. With these shares, projections of the future populations in each census tract could be obtained.

Using these data, the authors utilized a form of population potential modeling that alternatively employed population, households, traffic flows, and income to identify alternative trade areas for the sites and to determine the likely potential of the three sites relative to population flows and buying power. Based on

Box 8.1: Writing about Data

Observing some general rules will help the careful author of stories involving data achieve the writer's summit: clarity for the reader. Among them:

1. Do not stack your paragraphs with numbers. Few like to climb daunting hills, especially when the mountain is made of statistics. Use an anecdote, quote, or observation to separate paragraphs with lots of numbers. Remember that using more numbers minimizes the impact of other numbers. Generally speaking, do not have more than three figures of any kind in one sentence.

2. To have full meaning and context, a number must be compared to something. Its true meaning comes from its relative value. When using a statistic, compare it to something people can relate to, such as another time, an earlier year, or another place. Do not simply focus on a numeric increase or decrease, but also include the percentage change and how both compare with previous periods.

3. If a large, incomprehensible number is important to a story, make it meaningful. It will have a clearer meaning when the writer can supply an equivalent that's easier to visualize. A careful writer recasts as many numbers as possible in a simpler or more pictorial form that removes some of the abstraction that accompanies numbers. "Between 1980 and 1990, California gained more than six million people, more than the total population of all but 11 states."

4. Exact numbers may be required by real-estate brokers and other financial experts, but most readers do not need them. Round off large numbers and substitute them when it makes sense. For example, round the number 1,478,786 to 1.5 million. If something increased by 67.6 percent, a writer can say it went up by two-thirds. If it increased 98 percent, it almost doubled. Such expressions let the reader visualize.

5. Use ratios to simplify large numbers. Instead of saying that 261,389 students out of a total student population of 1,045,891 participate in the federally subsidized school breakfast program, say that one in four students partake of the program.

6. Know the source of statistics, the reputation of the provider, and the validity of the numbers. Know what they are quantifying and how they were computed. Read all data footnotes carefully.

7. Determine the significance of variance, whether any numeric or percentage changes are statistically significant.

8. Be careful not to mix apples and oranges, such as median and mean or constant and current dollars.

9. The most effective writing comes from selection, not compression, of facts. Choose only the numbers that have meaning to your readers. In a set of related numbers, decide what you want to say and construct a passage to say it as simply as possible.

10. Consider charting numbers instead of writing them. Removing them from the text not only improves your story, it often makes a bigger impression on readers.

11. Use comparable forms. "Three quarters of college students reported monthly alcohol use in 1990, compared with four-fifths in 1980."

12. Do not force readers to do their own math to figure out what you're saying. In fact, depending on sample size, an apparent difference may be a statistical artifact.

13. For many news developments, you only need one hard number. Everything else can be expressed in terms of comparison with that base.

14. Express things in ordinal terms—explain that some things are bigger or smaller than others without necessarily explaining exactly how much bigger or smaller in the same sentence.

both the number of persons in close proximity to the sites and with even greater emphasis on the income structure of the populations in the three site areas, the authors recommended the site in the university town. It was on the edge of a neighborhood occupied primarily by senior faculty members with higher incomes and was in close proximity to student dorms, which should provide substantial traffic in incidental purchases.

The company was very impressed with the report. It contained more than 100 pages of tables with an elaborate discussion of the literature on site selection and a detailed discussion of the data employed and the methods utilized. As a result of the analysis, the company purchased the site in the university community and built its convenience store at that location.

The initial enthusiasm with the selected site soon dissipated as the expected sales for the store failed to materialize. Both the owners and the authors were at a loss to understand why business was falling so far behind projections until one of the authors on a business trip happened to stop at one of the owners' stores in East Texas. He noticed that the store tended to stock items more appropriate to a rural low-income clientele. Heavy baked goods, microwave-based sandwiches, and non-diet colas were prominently displayed. The authors subsequently visited the troubled store and found a similar set of merchandise. The authors then entered into a very pointed discussion with the owners about their merchandising patterns. The owners were critical of the authors for failing to recognize the characteristics of what the owners felt were typical convenience stores and the authors were guilty of a very basic failing—they did not take the time to get to know their audience's (i.e., the client's) business. The client's business was not typical of convenience stores nationwide or in Texas, and the authors should have ensured that what they were examining was what the owners thought they were examining. It was also an unfortunate example of miscommunication because neither the owners nor the authors carefully explained their basic assumptions about the nature of the business that would be operated at the site.

The owners subsequently altered their product mix and the store was more successful, but the lessons are clear. Know your audience, know what is needed and what is wanted by the client, and make sure that what you plan to do is what is needed by the client—not simply what you want to do. Make sure that the client does not get lost in the data. If the report had been simpler and less numerically extensive, and if major points had been made in a clearly understandable way, the owners would have discovered that what was being analyzed was different from what they intended. For example, the detailed analysis made very clear the assumed income levels for patrons and which income levels were projected to produce a majority of the sales for the store. Had this been more clearly communicated to the owners in a way that indicated to them the relative income categories of those in the site areas versus those in the rest of Texas or East Texas, if careful comparisons had been provided by the authors, the misunderstandings could have been avoided. This case indicates that you can have the right data and use sophisticated methods but still analyze the data incorrectly for the intended uses.

Determining the Market for a Long-Term Care Facility
A market determination analysis conducted by demographers at a large land-grant university provides another useful example of the subtleties of using demographic data in a real-life setting. These demographers contracted with a small health care services firm that had decided to purchase a rural nursing home. The company wished to expand into the area of long-term care, and because the federal government was providing low interest loans for owners purchasing and operating such firms in underserved areas, it thought this particular home provided an excellent opportunity to enter the market with a reduced level of risk. The nursing home in question was a dominant one in its small market area, had contractual agreements with area hospitals for referrals, and had a long-term contract with the area's only licensed physician to provide care in the facility. Although the area in which the home operated was not showing extensive growth, it had a high proportion of elderly, particularly persons 75 years of age or older, the primary market segment requiring nursing home care. When the health services firm applied for the loan, however, the federal agency had its contracted consulting firm perform a market analysis for the home and, on the basis of that analysis, denied the loan. The company's owners were thoroughly familiar with the area and did not believe that the analysis provided to the federal agency was correct and so contracted with the demographers noted above to perform a separate market analysis. Making the analysis particularly challenging was the fact that the firm had only 45 days to contest the loan refusal and needed a completed market analysis in 30 days.

The analysts began by examining the report from the national consulting firm. The report appeared to be relatively complete and showed numerous patterns for the three-county market area that were verifiable using historic census data. In general, the study indicated that the three counties would have quite stable populations over the next several decades. This was a pattern that both the health firm's owners and the university team agreed was likely to prevail, but data available in the census and from other local sources did not seem to support the consulting firm's overall conclusion that the market for the nursing home was inadequate to make it profitable, and hence to have an acceptable level of risk to merit issuing a loan for its purchase.

What was particularly perplexing was the fact that the report showed projected rates of outmigration for persons over 60 and projected rates of inmigration for young adults. It suggested that a continuation of this pattern of elderly outmigration would erode the existing market for nursing home care and was a result of the fact that elderly persons were outmigrating from the area to access better health care facilities. Three things about this finding were surprising and appeared to be refuted by basic information on elderly migration patterns generally and data for the area in particular. First, demographic literature strongly suggests that elderly persons are less likely to migrate than younger residents (Weeks 2005). This same literature also suggests that rural elderly are particularly likely to remain in the areas in which they lived at earlier periods in their lives and shows that seeking health care is not a major contributor to elderly migration when it does occur; that is, most people believe that they have adequate care in the areas in which they live. In addition, data available from the United States Department of Agriculture and the State Data Center indicated that the counties in the market area had experienced little mobility of older persons but had experienced outmigration among young adults. The university analysts therefore concluded that the report provided by the consulting firm was likely flawed and sought additional information.

The university analysts contacted the firm that had completed the analysis for the federal agency asking for a complete report, including data used to make their market projections. The firm noted that it purchased its demographic data from another data provision firm and that firm noted that it provided historical demographic data but purchased its projections from a third firm. Beyond their basic conclusions in their reports, each firm refused to provide additional information saying that all additional information was proprietary. What was available was what was in the report provided to the agency and the proposed borrower. The university researchers knew some assumptions appeared to be inappropriate, but in the absence of more detailed data from the consulting firm, they could neither verify nor refute the consulting firm's findings.

To perform their own market analysis, the university analysts reviewed the literature on nursing home markets, obtained extensive data from the nursing home on the areas of residence, age, and other characteristics of their patients prior to entering the facility, gathered census data from Summary Files 1 and 3 from recent censuses, and obtained historical data and projections of the future population by age from the State Data Center in the state. They first verified the market area. The results suggested that the nursing home facility had captured a very large share (more than 90 percent) of the market in the county in which it was located, which was its primary market area, and roughly 20 percent of the market in the two other counties in the market area. The facility only occasionally admitted patients from any other areas.

The lack of growth in the overall market area population was eroding the overall population in the market area, but the population in place was quite old by comparative standards and appeared sufficient to provide a relatively stable market for the twenty-year period used in the evaluation by the loan provider. The market share was more problematic because approximately 100 residents were required in order for the facility to operate profitably. Projections indicated that the market share of the facility would have to remain at its current high rates in the primary market county and in the other secondary-market counties. Although there was nothing to indicate that there were any forces that would change the market share, the lack of room for any slippage in share was a factor that the researchers felt merited caution in making the investment and that they emphasized to the health services firm's owners.

The university analysts completed their analysis in less than a month and submitted it to the health services firm, which then submitted it to the federal agency. The agency reviewed the report and found it convincing and forwarded it to the consulting firm that had done the original analysis and asked them to reconsider its analysis. The firm redid its analysis and arrived at findings similar to those in the university's analysis. The agency indicated that it would reconsider the health services firm's application, and the firm immediately resubmitted it. During the agency's evaluation period, however, one of the market area's hospitals announced that it was closing, and the area's physician announced that he had accepted a position in another part of the state. Given the decline in potential referral sources and health care providers, the agency again declined the loan and the health services firm cancelled its plans to purchase the facility.

The example provides several important lessons. First, it again demonstrates the importance of obtaining a basic knowledge of demographic trends. The officials from the federal agency and owners of the health services firm did not have sufficient knowledge of migration patterns to know that the results reported by the consulting firm were highly unlikely. The university demographers did and thus knew exactly where to look for inconsistencies. In addition, the results show the importance of knowing data sources well. The researchers not only knew that the results from the consulting firm were unlikely, but also knew where to find data (in this case from the U.S. Department of Agriculture) that would allow them to assess the likely accuracy of the data. Similarly, knowledge of demographic data sources on general population patterns and of sources of population estimates and projections was clearly essential.

The results further point to the importance of obtaining and carefully selecting experts to help inform you in using data. The health services firm chose to consult not only persons who had expertise in demography but also those who also had expertise in the demography of rural areas and elderly persons. This selection was critical to the relatively quick turnaround provided by the professionals. This example also unfortunately demonstrates what is often a difficulty in using data from private data providers; that is, it was impossible to obtain sufficient information to know exactly what had been assumed in evaluating the data for the market area. Private data providers must have proprietary products if they are to remain profitable, but for the user this need can become problematic. As suggested above, we recommend that data produced with methodologies and sources for which the assumptions cannot be determined should not be used. Were we asked, we would have made this recommendation to the federal agency as well as the health services firm's owners.

Assessing Hiring Practices by a Defense Contractor

A small-scale technology company had successfully developed technology of utility to the U.S. Department of Defense (DOD). The company had been a very small firm with fewer than 25 employees, but as a result of the success of its new technology, it had increased its workforce to nearly 150 within a three-year period. After a high profile firing hit the press, however, the firm was asked by the DOD to indicate whether its hiring practices were in accordance with applicable employment laws governing firms receiving federal funds, such as those covered under the Equal Pay Act of 1963, the Age Discrimination in Employment Act of 1967, Title VII of the Civil Rights Act of 1964, and the Americans with Disability Act of 1990.

Because the firm had grown so rapidly, its human resources management had been less thorough than was desirable, and the company hired a human resources (HR) management firm that specialized in employment compliance analyses to prepare a report to comply with the DOD request. The firm was both familiar with the applicable laws and had extensive knowledge of the database produced for such purposes by the Census Bureau after each decennial census. This data file, called the Census 2000 Special EEO Tabulation, was developed by the Census Bureau under contract to the Equal Employment Opportunity Commission, the Department of Justice, the Department of Labor, and the Office of Personnel Management. It provides data for each county (and metropolitan areas, regions, the nation, etc.) on the number of workers by age, sex, and race/ethnicity (12–15 categories depending on the area) for 268 occupational groups. It thus allows for very detailed comparisons of a company's workforce with those in a company's labor market area.

The HR firm first determined the labor market area (in counties) for the firm drawing on proprietary data it had collected on employees in high-tech firms in the area. These data indicated which counties were appropriate for inclusion in the technology firm's market area. Then, in examining the job descriptions for the technology firm's employees, it became obvious that some were so specialized that the market was likely to be national in scope. The HR firm also found it difficult in some cases to align the technology company's own job titles with those covered by the EEO file. What was even more difficult was the fact that the technology company's HR records did not contain any indication of the race or ethnic origin of its employees. In the absence of such data, assessing the level of compliance with some federal regulations would be nearly impossible. It appeared that it would be necessary to have the technology firm gather race/ethnicity data for all employees, both past and present—a formidable and expensive process.

Further analysis by the HR firm, however, indicated that such data might not be necessary because the occupations represented in the technology firm's workforce were extremely specialized. An examination of these occupations for the labor market area applicable to the technology firm showed virtually no diversity by race/ethnicity or gender in the key occupational groups, and virtually all in the employment category were adults 20–35 years of age. Age, gender, and disability-related data items were in the technology company's personnel records, and the technology firm's labor force did closely match the age, gender, and disability characteristics of the general labor market workforce in its occupational categories. As a result, the HR firm completed a report for DOD stating that there was virtually no opportunity to create diversity in the technology firm's workforce, so the lack of race/ethnicity data was not a problem in assessing the company's compliance with applicable regulations.

Several months after the submission of the report, a DOD audit report was provided to the technology firm. It rejected the report's claims that an analysis by race/ethnicity was unnecessary. It ordered the technology firm to compile the data and complete a detailed analysis. The technology firm, with the assistance of the HR firm, completed the detailed reports with results that were not substantially different from those that the HR firm had argued it would obtain, due to the high degree of specialization of the workforce.

The lessons from this example are clear. Demographic data are often not only useful, but may be necessary under federal and other laws, and attention to demographic information is essential in the private as well as in the public sector. It also demonstrates that you can have a very skilled set of analysts who know the necessary data sets, you can complete sophisticated and detailed analyses, but you cannot overcome basic data inadequacies. Sometimes the data are simply not sufficient to the task, and appropriate (although, in this case, acceptable) conclusions could not be reached without the appropriate data. Data quality is key to effective analyses that adequately address important issues.

Governmental Uses and Misuses of Demographic Data

Although governmental uses and misuses of data are numerous, because of space limitations, we will provide only a single example of a government application. This example points to the difficulties that sometimes arise when the reality of data limitations meets the demands of policy.

Demographic Analyses in Water Use Planning
A statewide agency charged with water use planning was required by state legislation to complete a fifty-year water plan. The plan was to present projections of state-, regional-, county-, and place-level water demands taking into account both likely economic and population growth. The results of the projections (referred to

as forecasts by the agency) were to be reviewed by regional water authorities and consensus-based population and water-use projections developed for each region.

The task faced by the agency was a daunting one. Because the construction of water facilities and agreements for water rights require large-scale, long-term investments, planning horizons of fifty years were deemed necessary but were difficult given the state of knowledge in economic and demographic projections. The agency had to discern for fifteen regions of a rapidly economically diversifying state, with rapid but irregular patterns of population growth, what economic and demographic patterns would prevail in the state, regions, counties, and places for a fifty-year projection period. Such demands were clearly unreasonable given the state of knowledge in either economic or demographic projections because available scientific evidence suggest that projections for such long periods into the future are likely to be highly inaccurate. Because accuracy decreases for smaller-sized (in population terms) areas, projections for all of the state's nearly 1,000 places (many of which had fewer than 1,000 people) were particularly likely to be fraught with error. The reality, however, was that the law required that these projections be done, and the agency's economists and demographers were charged with doing what the law required.

The division charged with doing the projections assembled an advisory group of applied economists and demographers. All members of the advisory group expressed skepticism about the completion of such detailed projections for such long periods of time but also recognized that, for those in applied settings, what is required by policy and law may vary from that which is scientifically desirable or even reasonable. The advisory group worked with the staff of the water agency. It drew on previous econometric models for the state and made suggestions about their regionalization and suggested that the economic-demographic interface be done through applying the age- and sex-specific fertility and mortality rates used in projections by the state demographer with migration estimates based on regional population-to-employment ratios projected forward based on past trends and the mix of industries in a region. It also computed ratios of place populations to county populations for several census periods. In completing these steps, the advisory group drew on economic and demographic data from the most recent census (from SF1, SF2, and SF3), economic forecasts from the state comptroller's office, vital statistics data from the department of health, and fertility and mortality rates computed from the census and vital statistics data.

The major debates among the staff and advisory group members centered on what should be used to project the rates used in the analysis over a fifty-year time frame. What would the industrial structure be like fifty years into the future? How would technology alter productivity such as to change the population-to-employment ratios? How would fertility and mortality levels change over time and at what levels could current declines in fertility and mortality be expected to stabilize? How would residential and industrial water uses change over time as technology and resource bases changed? How would all of these factors vary by region and by county and place within regions? Obviously, these patterns were nearly impossible to identify for half a century into the future.

Despite such debates, the group (advisory and staff members) finally reached a consensus on (or in some cases at least a majority agreed to) certain assumptions. The industrial mix was deemed to continue trends that resulted in a diversified economy for each region at the level found in the most technologically sophisticated region of the state (based on percentages of the workforce employed in given industries) and then to remain at that level for the remainder of the projection period. Fertility levels were assumed to continue to decline for all racial/ethnic groups and to stabilize at a total fertility rate that was the lowest recorded to date for any Western nation in the world (about 1.4 births per woman). Longevity was assumed to increase such that the average life expectancy of all persons would approach ninety years and remain stable thereafter. Population-to-employment ratios were projected to change in accordance with historical patterns and stabilize at the levels found in the most technologically sophisticated region of the state at the beginning of the projection period. Historic trends in water use were assumed to follow patterns of increased conservation as deemed possible by agency engineers, and historic trends in shares for places within counties were projected forward assuming asymptotic trends in share models.

With substantial perseverance from the staff, projections of water demand were combined with hydrological data on potential water supplies, and a report was prepared showing statewide, regional, county, and place projections. It was extensive in size (more than 400 pages) and extensively documented. It was seen as providing projections that were as reasonable as possible given the policy and legislative requirements driving the analysis.

The legislation that required the analysis also required the development of projections that were agreed to by regional water boards. These boards were created by the legislation that created the planning processes and were composed of members appointed by the legislative leadership. The chief of staff for the agency's projection branch traveled across the state and was required to modify the projections as needed until there was a consensus on the projections between the agency and the board in each region. This involved an arduous 15-month process at the end of which the head of the projections branch retired. It also produced projections of population and economic activity substantially higher than those provided in the initial report, and the sum of the projections produced values higher than any reasonable projections that could be obtained by any separately produced statewide projections. Despite these problems, the official state projections for water planning purposes became those obtained by summing the regional values. The result was a set of projections of economic activity and population higher than nearly any applied economist or demographer in the state thought was reasonable.

The projections were nevertheless adopted by the statewide planning committee that advised the agency and are in effect today.

What lessons does this example provide to the user of demographic data and analysis? First, it shows the reality that often exists in applied analytical settings in government. Political and policy realities do not necessarily recognize the limits of science. The detail and time periods required in the projections were clearly not what the economic and demographic sciences suggested were reasonable, and clearly projections arrived at through a consensus between technical and nontechnical practitioners are likely to be problematic. Those who drafted the legislation, however, were heavily influenced by engineers and believed that longer-term projection periods would produce better water plans that could be more reasonably accommodated relative to engineering and fiscal requirements. In addition, extensive discussions with the drafters of the bill also suggested that they were as interested in creating the recognition of the need for, and initiation of, water use planning processes as they were in the outcome of the planning. No systematic water planning or management had been previously implemented at the state level, and even if the projections were likely to be inadequate and inaccurate, they could be updated periodically. At least a planning process was initiated in an area in which there had previously been no planning. Frankly, the drafters were also of the opinion that the economic and demographic sciences were incapable of producing accurate projections for any period of time so that extending the projections periods was unlikely to make the projections any more inaccurate than they would be anyway. A major lesson from this example is that the context of demographic analyses in the area of policy development often involves other than technical issues. This reality does not mean that less rigorous technical methods should be employed, but rather that realistic expectations about the use of such methods must be recognized in evaluating the utility of the processes.

What is unfortunate, however, is that there was no interaction between the policy-makers and the analysts prior to the drafting of the legislation. Had such consultation occurred, it is likely that different, more reasonable requirements would have been mandated. This example suggests that those using demographic data and analyses in applied settings would be well served by early involvement of data experts in the policy process.

Conclusions

The examples in this chapter show just how extensive are the uses of demographic data and how the context of their use affects the results of their use. They also suggest that even when the results produce questionable outcomes relative to the specific business decisions or policy requirements desired, the data are of critical importance in informing the decision-making processes. They suggest that demographic data and analyses, though imperfect, are clearly useful.

Chapter 9

Summary and Suggestions for Maintaining and Expanding Your Knowledge Base

Summary

In this volume, we have attempted to provide media, business, and governmental users who employ demographic data and analyses in their reporting and decision making with practical information on locating and effectively using demographic data. We have provided an overview of the content of demography and demographic analyses; a summary of demographic terms, concepts, measures, and methods of analyses; and an introduction to federal, state, and local sources of demographic information. Finally we have provided examples of such data in use in the media, business, and government.

In presenting this information, we have examined a wide range of dimensions and issues. The beginning chapters provided definitions for such key terms as "demography," "demographics," and "population" and the definitions and substantive content of the key demographic dimensions of size, fertility, mortality, migration, and population distribution. The key components of demographic characteristics such as age, sex, race/ethnicity, households, families, marriage, economic activity, educational attainment, and industry and occupational definitions were presented and discussed. The components of census geography from the block to the nation as a whole were identified, and the care that must be shown in measuring them and following change in them over time were emphasized.

The work provided an overview of selected demographic measures and methods. It emphasized that those presented are not meant to provide an exhaustive overview of such items but rather of ones likely to be encountered by analysts who are not professional demographers. Simple measures of each of the major demographic processes, dimensions, and characteristics were delineated as well as more elaborate procedures such as life table construction and methods for controlling for the effects of population composition.

Selected national, state, local, and private-sector sources of data were presented and evaluated. Included were key data items from the U.S. Bureau of the Census, the U.S. Bureau of Labor Statistics, the National Centers for Health and Educational Statistics, and a variety of other organizations and agencies. The importance of understanding the coverage and content of data items provided by such sources was noted in these discussions.

A major part of the text was devoted to how to accurately and effectively use demographic data once it is located. Principles for accurately and appropriately using and effectively presenting such data, and for interpreting it, were discussed.

These principles emphasized the importance of knowing your audience, knowing the subject matter, carefully preparing materials for presentation, using graphical presentations of materials, recognizing the significance of context, revealing the limitations of data, and providing a balanced presentation. The importance of making sure that you have the most appropriate measures of what you wish to measure; of taking into account measurement and sampling errors; of ensuring that you are making valid comparisons through such data; of using data for similar areas for similar items for similar time periods to interpret data's significance and relative importance; and the importance of attaining basic knowledge of demographic trends so you can properly interpret and describe the significance and importance of such data were also discussed.

Finally, the text provided examples of the use of demographic data in the media, business, and government. This section attempted to provide a sense of the problems and opportunities encountered in using demographic data to address real-world issues in applied settings.

In sum, although no single volume can be inclusive of all that you might need to know to do an exhaustive demographic study or analysis, this volume has attempted to provide an overview of some of the most critical dimensions required in using and completing a valid analysis with demographic data. We have suggested that in the absence of attention to such factors as those noted in the chapters in this volume, data are likely to be misused and misinterpreted, sometimes with disastrous effects relative to accuracy and to arriving at the best private- or public-sector decisions. Hopefully the importance of understanding and using data appropriately has become apparent and you have gained knowledge that will help you use demographic data more accurately and with greater effectiveness.

Suggestions for Maintaining and Expanding Your Knowledge Base

Where do you go from here? In a sense this volume is like a technical manual that you can read to learn about demographic data, analysis techniques, sources, and the appropriate means of accurately and effectively using such data. But, reading about it is different from putting it into practice. The best way to learn about locating demographic data is to try to locate such data for specific uses. The best means of learning how a demographic measure is computed and how it can be used is to compute it for areas with which you are familiar. The most effective way to learn how to appropriately use demographic data is to actually employ it to address your own reporting, business, or governmental needs. Practice is required to obtain the necessary skills to locate, use, and analyze demographic data.

In addition to practicing demographic data use and analyses, there are several general practices that can be usefully pursued to maintain and expand your demographic skills.

Become a Regular User of the Census Bureau's and Your State Data Center's Web Sites

The Census Bureau and your State Data Center provide ongoing analyses of demographic trends affecting the nation and your state. Bookmarking these sites and checking them a couple of times a week is an easy way of increasing your knowledge base relative to demographic data and of gaining substantive knowledge of demographic trends for the nation and states. Equally important, such sites will often refer you to other data that are likely to be of relevance and provide you with information that will allow you to contact national, state, and local demographic experts (for example, the Census Bureau Web site's list of the representatives of State Data Centers and Federal State Cooperatives for Population Estimates and Projections). Members of the press may wish to also become recipients of embargoed press releases from the Census Bureau's Web site and can obtain information on doing so by contacting the Public Information Office at the U. S. Bureau of the Census.

Subscribe to a Few Demographic Publications

You may also want to subscribe to a few demographic publications (most of which are now available online) that can help keep you abreast of current developments. Although there are numerous ones available, we believe many users will find products and publications from two organizations of particular interest. One such source is the Population Reference Bureau, which provides an online set of services and produces periodic bulletins that call attention to major demographic trends related to such factors as household size, immigration, and poverty. It also provides reports on the demographics of nations and regions of the world (e.g., in China, Mexico, Europe), and examinations of the impacts of population change on economic, environmental, and other factors. It also produces annual data sheets showing key characteristics of all nations that are useful for comparative analyses. A publication with a more commercial focus is *American Demographics*. This publication provides overviews of demographic trends with an emphasis on their commercial and business implications. Both *American Demographics* and publications from the Population Reference Bureau are available by subscription, and their organizations can be contacted and subscriptions to key publications obtained online [http://www.adage.com/section.cms?sectionId=195 and http://www.prb.org/]. There are, of course, numerous other publications that may be helpful, ranging from the popular to scientific journals in demography. Among the latter are *Demography, Population and Development Review, Social Biology,* and *Population Research and Policy Review.* These are technical journals that are intended for professional demographers and thus may, or may not, be useful to users involved in other types of demographic data use or analyses.

Network with Other Demographic Data Users

It is also useful to network with others who do what you do. Many metropolitan areas have data user groups that meet monthly, quarterly, or annually; professionals in business have their professional organizations where some will be involved in similar activities; and there are national groups as well. One such group is the Applied Demography section of the Population Association of America (PAA). The PAA is the major nationwide professional organization for demographers, and the Applied Demography group in it is made up primarily of business and state and local government demographers and some demographers with major emphases in media and communication. Such groups generally have low-cost memberships and can help you remain current on demographic data and trends.

Attend or Audit a Demography Course at a Community College or University

For those who are very interested in the subject matter of demography, auditing or simply asking permission to attend an introductory demography course at a local college or university can be an excellent way to gain a basic level of knowledge about demographic trends. Such courses usually cover historic, current, and projected international and national population patterns and examine the implications of population change for political, social, environmental, economic, and commercial dimensions. Even if you cannot attend all the lectures and read all the readings, you can obtain a substantial level of knowledge with a relatively modest investment of time. If such an experience increases your interest substantially, more formal educational opportunities are available. Most universities with a graduate program will have courses on methods of demographic analyses and on such subareas within demography as fertility, mortality, and migration.

Do Not Limit Your Level of Knowledge to the Minimum Necessary to Survive

There is an old saying that someone knows just enough to be dangerous. Such a state of knowledge is very dangerous in the area of demographic data use and analysis. It is critical that you obtain a sufficient working knowledge of demographic data and analysis. As the examples in Chapters 6, 7, and 8 make evident, errors are likely to be made if you do not obtain an adequate level of knowledge, and some of these errors could be career-ending occurrences. On the other hand, appropriate use of demographic data can be critical in policy formation and in informing private-sector decision making. It is difficult to measure such adequacy, but if you repeatedly read materials from the general sources noted above and do not understand what is being written and do not know whether what is being written is reasonable relative to past trends or trends in similar areas, you need to build your knowledge base.

Conclusions

Demographics, like all other areas of knowledge, is constantly changing and evolving. You never will know it all, but you must ensure that you take the actions necessary to keep yourself sufficiently current to be effective in the basic use and analysis of demographic information. What we have attempted to do in this volume is to give you a starting point for obtaining the base of knowledge you will need to report on demographics and/or to use demographic data for public- or private-sector decision making. Recognize that this book is but a starting point, however, and that learning about demographics is part of an ongoing learning process that you have now only initiated.

Appendix A
Glossary of Major Demographic
Terms and Measures

Abortion Rate*: The number of abortions per 1,000 women ages 15–44 or 15–49 in a given year.

Administrative or Legal Geographic Entities: Areas recognized as political boundaries; areas originating from laws, treaties, charters, or court decisions. (Example: states and counties).

Age: For census data, the age of each person is based on his or her age in complete years on the date of the census, (for example, April 1, 2000). Alternative sources may derive age data from date of birth information. Age may be reported by single years, by age groups, or for larger categorized groups such as the voting age population (ages 18+), children (less than 18 years of age), school age children (ages 5–18), the elderly (ages 65+), or the working population (ages 16+).

Age-Sex Pyramid (or population pyramid): A graph constructed by taking the number of males and females of each age and graphing their numbers (see Figure 3.18). Traditionally, data for females are shown on the right and data for males are shown on the left of a paired-bar chart to produce this graph. Pyramids with large bases reveal populations that are generally younger and pyramids with more uniform sized distributions across ages usually indicate older populations.

Age-Specific Rate*: Rate obtained for specific age groups (for example, age-specific fertility rate, death rate, marriage rate, illiteracy rate, or school enrollment rate) (see Figure 3.4 and Figure 3.19).

American Community Survey (ACS): The Census Bureau's large-scale survey currently planned to replace the long form in the 2010 Census. It is an annual survey of 3 million households and will be used to estimate long-form characteristics at geographic levels as small as census block groups.

Ancestry: The country or countries to which a person traces his or her heritage. While the census allows respondents to report one or more ancestry groups, only the first two items are coded.

---

*   Starred items are all derived from the Population Reference Bureau's "Economic and Demographic Terms Glossary." 1998. In *Population Handbook*. 4th internat'l. ed.; and the U.S. Bureau of the Census.

Average: see *Mean*

Average Household Size: The number of persons living in households divided by the number of households. This value is usually expressed as average or mean "persons per household" for a given geographic area.

Block Group (BG): A statistical subdivision of a census tract that consists of all tabulation blocks whose numbers begin with the same digit (e.g., BG 4 contains all blocks numbered 4000–4999). Like census blocks, block groups are only unique within census tracts. In general, block groups range in size from 500 to 3,000 people with an optimal size of 1,500.

Bookkeeping Equation: see *Population Equation*

Caseload: The number of cases handled, usually restricted to a given time period and/or given geographic area. This term is frequently used in social services but can also be applied to other service areas.

Cause-Specific Death Rate*: The number of deaths attributable to a specific cause per 100,000 population in a given year.

Census Block: The smallest geographic area for which the Census Bureau tabulates data. This area is delineated on maps drawn by the Census Bureau with boundaries that may be physically visible and/or nonvisible features. In most cities they conform to the common perception of a block as a rectangular area bounded on four sides by four different streets. Block areas were renumbered for Census 2000 using 4-digit numbers; previously this geography was specified by 3-digit numbers. Block numbers are only unique within their census tracts. There is no population size criteria for a block.

Census Designated Place (CDP): A concentration of population, housing, and commercial structures that is identified by name but is not within an incorporated place. Its boundaries are determined by local-area data committees working with the Census Bureau.

Census Tract: A statistical subdivision of a county or county equivalent. Tract boundaries can follow physical features such as major roads or rivers, but invisible features such as governmental boundaries may also form tract boundaries. Tracts do not cross county or state boundaries. Although tracts are intended to be stable and the Census Bureau describes them as "relatively permanent," tract boundaries may be revised from decade to decade, especially in rapidly growing areas. They generally contain between 1,000 and 8,000 people with an average of 4,000.

Central Business District (CBD): The center of commercial activity in a city, this is often the largest and oldest concentration of commerce in the area. The boundaries of these areas are similar to urbanized areas designated by the Census Bureau in constituting its geography.

Central City: The largest place, or in some cases more than one place, in a Metropolitan Statistical Area (MSA) or Consolidated Metropolitan Statistical Area (CMSA). The largest central city and in some cases the names of up to two additional places are included in the Metropolitan Area (MA) title.

Child-Woman Ratio*: The number of children under age 5 per 1,000 women ages 15–44 or 15–49 in a population in a given year. This crude fertility measure, based on basic census data, is sometimes used when more specific fertility information is not available.

Citizenship and Foreign Born Status: Census data concerning citizenship and birth status are determined by answers to long-form questions. Respondents were asked to select their place of birth: "U.S. state," "Puerto Rico," "U.S. island area," or "foreign country." A separate question asks if the person is a citizen of the United States and whether that person is a citizen by birth or naturalization. No questions are asked regarding immigration status.

Cohort: A group of people born during the same time period and potentially having other common characteristics.

Congressional District (CD): One of the 435 areas from which people are elected to the U.S. House of Representatives. Following each decennial census, state legislatures have the responsibility for drawing new CD boundaries for states with two or more representatives.

Consolidated Metropolitan Statistical Area (CMSA): To be designated as a CMSA, an area must have a population of 1,000,000 or more, have component parts that qualify as PMSAs, and have the approval of local governments for the designation. Like other metropolitan areas, CMSAs are composed of whole county areas, except in New England where county subdivisions can delineate their boundaries.

Consumer Expenditures: Indicators providing information concerning the buying habits of consumers. Expenditure data are collected by the Bureau of Labor Statistics from a survey containing two parts, a two-week record-keeping survey with participants recording dollar amounts for goods and services purchased and a series of five interviews concerning expenditures conducted every three months (once per quarter) for five quarters. The Consumer Expenditure Survey also collects demographic data on participating consumer units that provide useful information on the buying habits among various population groups.

Consumer Price Index*: A concept developed by the U.S. Bureau of Labor Statistics. It is used to measure average changes in prices over time of a fixed market basket of goods and services. It is used as one measure of inflation.

County: The primary legal division in most states. States that do not have county divisions, such as Alaska and Louisiana, will have other types of county equivalent areas (boroughs and parishes) for data tabulation and presentation purposes.

Crude Birth Rate*: The number of live births per 1,000 population in a given year. Not to be confused with the growth rate (see Figure 3.2).

Crude Death Rate*: The number of deaths per 1,000 population in a given year (see Figure 3.2).

Current and Constant Dollars: Income and other financial data are closely related to their reporting date since the value of a dollar changes over time. Researchers should use caution in comparing such data between time periods; an amount recorded at a given point in time is said to be in current dollars, but if that value is adjusted to a reference year based on rates of inflation, then the value is in constant dollars.

Current Population Survey (CPS): Conducted by the Census Bureau for the Bureau of Labor Statistics, this national monthly survey of approximately 50,000 households is used to estimate employment and other characteristics. It provides the data reported in the P-20, P-23, and P-60 census publication series.

Demography: The study of population size, distribution, and composition and the processes that determine these, namely fertility, mortality, and migration, and the determinants and consequences of all of the above.

Demographics: A nontechnical term generally used to connote information and data on the size, geographic distribution, and characteristics of a population that affect its use of, its participation in, and/or its access to specific types of goods and services.

Density (population density): The number of people per square mile. In international statistics, density may be measured in other units of area, such as persons per square kilometer or hectare (see Figure 3.12).

Dependency Ratio: The number of persons in dependent ages relative to the number in working ages. Dependent ages typically include persons too young to work or in school (variously specified as ages 0–14 or 0–19) and those past their working years or retired (65 years of age or older). Persons in the ages defined as economically productive, or the working-age population, are those between the dependent ages (15–64 or 19–64 years of age) (see Figure 3.16).

Direct Standardization: see *Standardization*

Distribution: see *Population Distribution*

Divorce Rate (or crude divorce rate)*: The number of divorces per 1,000 population in a given year.

Doubling Time (or doubling period): The time necessary for a population to double in size.

Dropout Rate: These measures of educational completion can be calculated and reported using several different criteria. Schools and school districts are often required to report annually the number of public school dropouts divided by the number of students in the affected grades for the same year. Grades reported often include grades 7–12, grades 9–12 or grades 11 and 12. The National Center for Education Statistics defines a dropout as a student in grades 9–12 who was enrolled in school but does not return to public school the following fall, who is not expelled, did not continue school elsewhere, did not graduate or otherwise complete school, or died.

Earnings: The sum of all regularly received income and wages, including self employment income *before* deductions for taxes, social security, or other withdrawals.

Education: Measures of education include the educational attainment for adult populations and educational enrollment for those still attending educational institutions. While educational involvement can involve persons of any age, measures of enrollment commonly begin at ages 3 or 5 and extend to 35 years of age. While there is no terminal age for the completion of one's education, educational attainment is typically measured for persons 18 years of age or older and for persons 25 years of age and older.
  - **Educational Attainment** reports the highest level of education attained by a person. The census collects and reports the educational attainment both for persons 18 years of age and older as well as for persons 25 years of age and older with detail on level achieved.

- **Educational Status** is the level of education for a population, defined in terms of attainment in levels or years of school completed or average number of years of education.

- **Enrollment Status** is collected on the census long form for individuals currently enrolled in a regular school or college and is reported for persons 3 years of age and older. Enrollment is also reported by the type of school attended, "public" or "private."

Enrollment: Work-related activity that results in the attainment of resources (income) for the person or persons involved. Measures of employment include a person's labor force status ("employed" or "unemployed"), as well as descriptive characteristics concerning the duration and type of employment (such as part-time or full-time, occupation, and industry of employment). Census 2000 asked employment status for population 15 years of age or older, but tables derived for employment variables are provided for persons 16 years of age or older.

Employment Status (or labor force status): Classified in a hierarchical mode by the census, population ages 16 and older are first classified as "in labor force" or "not in labor force." Those persons who are in the labor force are then classified as "in armed forces" or "civilian." Finally, those in the civilian labor force are classified as "employed" or "unemployed."

Exponential Change: A measure of population change that assumes continuous compounding. This measure of change simulates the constant additions (through births and inmigration) and deletions (through deaths and outmigration) occurring in populations (see Figure 3.5).

Family*: Two or more persons living together and related by birth, marriage, or adoption. Families may consist of siblings or other relatives as well as married couples and any children they have.

Fertility: The reproductive behavior (specifically the number of births) in a population.

Foreign Born: In the United States, the foreign born population includes all persons who were not U.S. citizens at birth. Foreign born persons are either citizens due to naturalization or are not U.S. citizens. These are first generation immigrants identified by their country of birth.

Gender: see *Sex and Gender*

General Fertility Rate*: The number of live births per 1,000 women ages 15–44 or 15–49 years in a given year (see Figure 3.3).

Gini Coefficient: A measure of inequality expressed as a number between "0" (corresponding to perfect equality) and "1" (corresponding to perfect inequality). A **Gini Index** provides the Gini Coefficient expressed as a percentage. While frequently used to measure income inequality, the Gini Coefficient also measures other forms of uneven distributions between two factors (see Figure 3.15).

Gross Reproduction Rate (GRR)*: The average number of daughters that would be born alive to a woman (or group of women) during her lifetime if she passed through her childbearing years conforming to the age-specific fertility rates of a given year. See also total fertility rate.

Group Quarters: Persons who do not live in housing units are classified by the Census Bureau as living in group quarters. Two types of group quarters are recognized, including institutional and noninstitutional.
- **Institutionalized** group quarters populations include persons under supervised care or custody in institutions during the census. Classified as "patients" or "inmates," these persons are restricted to the institution grounds.
- **Noninstitutionalized** group quarters populations are persons living in group quarters other than institutionalized facilities, such as college dormitories, military barracks, or homeless shelters.

High School Completion Rate: The National Center for Educational Statistics (NCES) completion rate reports the percentage of persons 18 to 24 years of age who have left high school and earned a high school diploma either through graduation or General Educational Development (GED).

Household*: An occupied housing unit and all persons who occupy that housing unit. A household may be comprised of one or more families, one or more unrelated individuals, or a combination of families and unrelated individuals.

Household Type: Households are classified *by type* according to the sex of the householder and by the presence of relatives in the household.
- A **family household** or **family** is a householder living with one or more persons who are related to him or her by birth, marriage, or adoption.
- A **nonfamily household** is a householder living alone or with other nonrelatives.

All families are households but not all households are families.

Householder (formerly head of household): One person in each household is designated as the householder (Person 1 - when completing the census form), this is usually the person in whose name the home is owned, being bought, or is rented. If there is no such person, any household member who is over 15 years of age can be designated as the householder by the person responding to the census.

Housing Units: Separate living quarters in which the occupants live separately from any other individuals in the building. A housing unit may be a house, an apartment, a mobile home, a group of rooms, or a single room that can be occupied as separate living quarters.

Incidence Rate*: The number of persons contracting a disease per 1,000 population at risk, for a given period of time.

Income: Income refers to money received from any source. For the purposes of census data collections, persons are asked to report their income for the calendar year prior to the date of the census; therefore, all 2000 Census data related to income and poverty reference 1999 incomes. The American Community Survey (ACS), which will replace the long form of the census by 2010, asks for income in the last twelve months (from the day the survey is received). As for employment data, questions concerning income on the 2000 Census were asked of persons 15 years of age or older, but tabulations are provided for persons 16 years of age and older. Income can be reported by different means, the three most common measures being per capita income, mean income, and median income.

- **Aggregate personal or household income** refers to the total income of all persons or households in a population.
- **Income of households** sums the income of the householder and any other individuals 15 years of age or older in the housing unit whether they are related to the householder or not.
- **Income of families** sums the income of the householder and any other individuals 15 years of age or older in the household who are related to the householder.
- **Individual income** is the sum of all types of income for each person 15 years or older.
- **Per capita income** is the average or mean income per person in an area (including minors and all nonearners).
- **Mean income** is the average income, which can be computed per household or per family in an area by dividing the total income by the number of households or families.
- **Median income** is the income value from a ranked list of incomes for persons, households, or families in an area that divides the list into equal halves (for households, this figure would indicate that half of the

households have a higher income than the median, and half the households have lower incomes than the median).

Incorporated Places: Governmental units incorporated under a state's laws, such as a city, town, borough, or village, to provide governmental services for people within established legal boundaries.

Index of Dissimilarity (ID): A measure of distribution that indicates the similarity of two categorical percentage distributions, calculated as one-half the sum of the absolute differences between the percentage values in the categories of the two distributions. The index varies between "0" (corresponding to perfect equality) and "1" (corresponding to perfect inequality). This measure indicates the proportion of a population that would have to change categories for the two distributions to be identical. The ID is sometimes referred to as the **Segregation Index** due to its application in measuring segregation of racial/ethnic groups in cities and other areas (see Figure 3.15).

Indirect Standardization: see *Standardization*

Industry: The industry or type of business an employed person participates in. Like occupations, industry classifications are organized hierarchically in a coded system and are revised when necessary. Census codes for industry groups utilized in the 2000 Census are based upon the 1997 North American Industry Classification System (NAICS). This classification system was completely revised from the previous Standard Industrial Classification (SIC) System used prior to 1997, such that anyone using industry data from an earlier period must be aware of the substantial changes in the classifications before and after 1997. While SIC to NAICS crosswalks are available online, many industrial classifications are not comparable between these two systems, making 1990 to 2000 intercensal analyses nearly impossible for many industries.

Infant Mortality: The number of deaths occurring to persons less than one year of age.
- **Neonatal mortality** refers to deaths of infants less than one month old.
- **Postneonatal mortality** refers to deaths of infants from one month to one year old.

Infant Mortality Rate: The number of infant deaths (deaths to persons less than one year of age) divided by the number of births for a given year multiplied by a constant (see Figure 3.7). Infant mortality is often examined in terms of the following two components:
- **Neonatal death rates** are calculated for infants less than one month old.

- **Postneonatal death rates** are calculated for infants one month to one year of age.

Labor Force*: All persons 16 years old and older who are either employed or unemployed, but are actively looking for work and available to accept employment, plus the members of the Armed Forces.

Labor Force Participation Rates (see Figure 3.19):
- **Crude Labor Force Participation Rate (CLFPR)** refers to the labor force population divided by the total population and multiplied by a constant.
- **General Labor Force Participation Rate (GLFPR)** refers to the labor force population divided by the economically active population (usually 15–64 or 20–64 years of age) multiplied by a constant. Commonly referred to as the labor force participation rate.
- **Age-Specific Labor Force Participation Rate (ASLFPR)** refers to the labor force population in age group "A" divided by the population in age group "A" multiplied by a constant.

Less Developed Countries*: Following United Nations definitions, the term "less developed countries" (or "regions") refers to countries in Africa, Asia (except Japan), Latin America and the Caribbean, and Oceania (except Australia and New Zealand).

Life Expectancy: The average remaining years of life at a given age. This term most commonly refers to the life expectancy at birth, or the total average number of years a person might expect to live.

Life Span*: The maximum age that human beings could reach under optimum conditions.

Life Table: A table derived by applying a given set of age-specific mortality rates to a population (of 100,000) over the entire lifetime of the population. This table simulates how many persons die at each age until the last person in the population dies. See Figure 3.8 for an example of a life table and Figure 3.9, which briefly defines the standard elements of life tables. Also see single-decrement life tables and multiple-decrement life tables in this appendix. See Figure 3.21 for an explanation of common components in multiple-decrement life tables.

Living Quarters: Accommodations including either housing units or group quarters. Most living quarters are dwellings intended for residential use, but the term may also refer to tents, vans, emergency shelters, dormitories, and barracks.

Lorenz Curve: A line chart showing a graphical representation of two cumulative percentage distributions (represented by a curved line) compared to a line of perfect equality (represented by a straight line). This type of distribution chart is often used to measure income inequality (see Figure 3.14).

Marital Status: In Census 2000, persons were asked to self identify their status as "Now married," "Divorced," "Separated," or "Never married" on a long-form question tabulated for the population 15 years of age and older. This question also asked "spouse present" or "spouse absent" to clarify the living arrangements for the household.

Market Area: The territory surrounding a central point of exchange that includes all potential customers for whom market price and transport cost would be acceptable for them to be willing to purchase a commodity or services at a given price at that central point.

Marriage Rate (or crude marriage rate)*: The number of marriages per 1,000 population in a given year.

Mean (or average): The arithmetic average widely used to measure demographic and socioeconomic factors such as mean age at first marriage or average size of household. It is computed by summing the values of interest (such as household income for all households) and dividing the sum by the number of cases (e.g., households).

Median: The value that divides a ranked distribution in half (with 50% above and 50% below the median value). This measure is commonly utilized to describe median age of a population or median income level.

Metadata: Information describing characteristics of a data set, such as sources, content, and any quality or condition issues.

Metropolitan Area (MA): The federal Office of Management and Budget defines large population centers and their adjacent counties that share economic and social integration with the center as metropolitan areas. The definitions applied to metropolitan areas have changed over time; and following each decennial census, the areas within different types of metropolitan areas are reallocated. Metropolitan areas generally are composed of counties or county equivalents with a central city of 50,000 or more people and counties around this central city county that have a high degree of interaction with the central city county as measured by commuting.

Metropolitan Statistical Area (MSA): A metropolitan area that is not closely associated with another MA and is considered as an independent entity is defined as an MSA. Each MSA must have at least one urbanized area with a population of 50,000 or more and include one or more counties or county equivalents. New England is an exception to the county rule, as its MSAs are defined in terms of county subdivisions.

Microdata: Term used by the census to refer to special samples that involve samples of individual households' surveys compiled for detailed analytical purposes with special procedures used to protect confidentiality.

Micropolitan Statistical Area: An area with at least one urban cluster with between 10,000 and 50,000 people. A Micropolitan Statistical Area includes the central county or counties including the core city or cities, plus any adjacent counties with a high degree of social and economic interaction with the central county.

Migration: The movement of people from one area to another area with the intent of the move being to establish a relatively permanent change in residence. In the United States persons who move from one county to another are called **migrants** (see migration rate formulas in Figure 3.10).

- **Inmigration** refers to the movement of people into a reference area in the United States (persons moving in are **inmigrants**).
- **Outmigration** refers to the movement of people out of a reference area in the United States (persons moving out are **outmigrants**).
- **Net migration** is the difference between the migration into an area and the migration out of the same area.
- **Domestic** or **internal migration** refers to persons moving and changing residence within the same country.
- **International migration** refers to persons moving between countries. Also sometimes referred to by the general term of immigration.
- **Immigration** refers to the movement of persons into a reference nation from another nation.
- **Immigration rate** refers to the number of persons moving into a reference nation per 1,000 population in the reference nation during a given time period (usually one year).
- **Emigration** refers to the movement of persons out of a reference nation.
- **Emigration rate** refers to the number of persons moving out of a reference nation per 1,000 population in the reference nation during a given time period (usually one year).
- **Net immigration** is the difference between population moving into a reference nation and those moving out of that reference nation.

Mobility*: The geographic movement of people. Such persons are called movers. Generally movers travel shorter distances than migrants.

Mode: A statistical measure indicating the value occurring most often. This measure can be utilized to describe patterns of frequency such as the most common occupation or industry of employment for an area.

Mortality: The incidence of deaths in a population.

Multiple-Decrement Life Table: A life table showing the impacts of mortality plus one or more additional factors on a population. Examples of such tables include nuptiality tables, school life tables, and working life tables (see Figure 3.21).

Natural Increase: The numerical difference between the number of births and deaths, also called "natural change."

Neighborhood: An enclave is an area in a city that is distinguished from adjoining areas by common characteristics of the population living there.

Numeric Change: A common measure of population change between two time periods. For population this is the difference obtained by subtracting the number of persons at an earlier period of time from the number at a later period of time.

Occupation: A measure of the employed labor force by the type of job held (what a person does). Occupations are grouped hierarchically in a coded system that has been revised over time but is currently based on the 2000 Standard Occupational Classification System (SOC). While the Census Bureau utilizes its own occupation codes, they are based on the SOC system.

Percent Change: A common measure of population change between two time periods, stated as a percentage of the base population. Percent population change is computed by subtracting the number of people at an earlier period of time from the population at a later period of time, then dividing the difference by the population at the earlier period and multiplying the result by 100 (see Figure 3.1).

Place of Birth: Data collected by the U.S. Census Bureau on its long questionnaire that asks where the person was born. For persons born in the United States, the state of birth is requested. For persons born outside of the United States, the name of a country or the U.S. territorial area (e.g., Puerto Rico, Guam) is requested.

Population: A population consists of the persons living in a specific geographical area at a specific point in time. It refers to the aggregate, the group of people as a whole, in an area.

Population Composition: The characteristics of a population. Composition describes a population by such characteristics as age, sex, race/ethnicity, income, and education.

Population Density: The number of people per unit of land area. In the United States this is generally per square mile. In international statistics, density is usually computed as persons per square kilometer or hectare (see Figure 3.12).

Population Distribution: The description of how people in a population are distributed relative to the physical space or land area that the population inhabits (see Figure 3.13, Figure 3.14, and Figure 3.15).

Population Equation: A simple means of characterizing the components of population change: that is $P_{t_2} = P_{t_1} + B_{t_1-t_2} - D_{t_1-t_2} + M_{t_1-t_2}$ where P refers to population, B refers to births, D refers to deaths, M refers to net migration, and t_1 and t_2 refer to earlier and later time periods, respectively.

Population Estimate: Approximation of the size, and potentially other, characteristics of a population for periods of time between the last census and the present time. Common techniques for estimating population include the following:
- **Extrapolation techniques** assume that the numerical increase from past periods (such as the last intercensal period) will continue from the date of the last census to the estimate date or that past rates will continue to the estimate date.
- **Symptomatic techniques** view the changes in various population indicators as indicative (symptomatic) of population change. The **housing unit method** is a good example of a symptomatic technique, as indicators of new housing units, vacancies, and/or demolitions can be employed to estimate population changes in a given area.
- **Regression-based techniques** are similar to symptomatic techniques except that they use regression methods based on multiple symptoms with the relative weight of each estimator in the determination of the total population being derived from historical data.
- **Component techniques** estimate the components of population change (births, deaths, and net migration) and then use these estimates to determine the estimate of population, rather than estimating the population size directly. When components for births, deaths, and migration are

prepared for particular cohorts of the population, these become **cohort-component methods,** which are very useful in providing estimates of population characteristics such as age, sex, race/ethnicity, etc.

Population Potential: A measure of population distribution relative to two or more sites, this indicates the number of persons for whom each of a given number of alternative geographic locations is the most accessible. This measure of population distribution is often used for site selection analyses (see Figure 3.13).

Population Projection: Approximation of the size and potentially other characteristics of a population for future periods of time. Projections utilize assumptions about future populations or future patterns for demographic processes. Commonly used techniques for projecting populations include:

- **Extrapolative, curve-fitting, and regression-based techniques** utilize past numerical or rates of growth or patterns of growth to project future populations. They usually assume that annual or multiyear values, rates, or patterns of growth will continue from the last census to the projection date.
- **Ratio-based techniques** utilize projections for a larger area (of which the projection area is a part) projecting population for the smaller projection area based on its proportion of the larger area's population for the projection period.
- **Land-use techniques** are often used to determine growth potential for smaller areas, since large areas such as counties and states are less likely to be significantly affected by land-use patterns. These techniques include methods for projecting when an area has reached its optimum size (usually based on population density) or if its land use makes future settlement unlikely either because the area is undesirable (such as in a flood zone, near a landfill or sewage treatment plant, etc.) or not accessible (unuseable terrain, park areas, etc.).
- **Economic-based techniques** assume that population change is largely a product of economic change; if the number of jobs increases, the number of people will increase. This method usually is tied to assumptions of econometric models projecting future growth and development using some form of population-to-employment ratio.
- **Cohort-component techniques** utilize age (and sometimes sex and race/ethnicity) cohorts with historical rates of fertility, mortality, and migration (i.e., the components) for each cohort and assumptions about future patterns of component change by cohort to project populations by cohort.

Population Pyramid: see *Age-Sex Pyramid*

Population Size: The number of people in a population.

Poverty: The absence of wealth. Measures of poverty are derived from income data for families and unrelated individuals. A two-dimensional matrix presents income thresholds for unrelated individuals and two-person families (also differentiated by over 65 years of age or under 65 years of age) and categorized for families based on family size and number of children present. Persons or families with incomes falling below the income threshold for their specified size of family unit are considered in poverty.

Poverty Rate: The percentage of persons, households, or families in poverty of all persons, households, or families for whom poverty status is determined.

Primary Metropolitan Statistical Area (PMSA): In MSAs with a population of 1,000,000 or more persons (referred to as Consolidated Metropolitan Areas), two or more Primary Metropolitan Statistical Areas may be defined. Certain official standards must be met and local governments must accept the designation.

Principal City: Following the 2000 Census, metropolitan areas were redefined with new guidelines from the Office of Management and Budget. In the current definition used (beginning in 2003), the largest city in each MSA or CMSA is designated a principal city. MSAs or CMSAs may have more than one principal city if specified requirements are met regarding population size and employment. The title of each MA includes the names of up to three of the principal cities and is based on cities' populations.

Public Use Microdata Area (PUMA): Geographic area designed to be utilized with Public Use Microdata Sample (PUMS) files. The PUMS files allow data users to access microdata to create their own tabulations and data summaries. To maintain respondent confidentiality these tabulations are only allowed for areas of a certain population size. PUMAs designated for the 5 percent PUMS sample must have a minimum population of 100,000. For the 1 percent PUMS sample a minimum census population of 400,000 is required.

Race and Ethnicity: "Race" and "ethnicity" are frequently utilized together to refer to differences among populations related to their cultural, historical, or national-origin characteristics. Although the concept of race was once assumed by some segments of some societies to describe a base of biological differences, race has come to indicate differences that are largely socioeconomic and cultural. Ethnicity generally refers to the national, cultural, or ancestral origins of a people. As used in the U.S. Census of Population and Housing, all designations of race and ethnicity are self-identified by respondents to the census. They are not verified by the census taker. Race is determined by a question that asks the respondent to indicate whether he or she and every other member of the household is White, Black or African American, Asian, American Indian or Alaskan Native, Native Hawaiian or Pacific Islander, or a member of some Other racial group. Ethnicity is determined from a separate question that asks the respondents to indicate for themselves and all other members of the household whether they are of Hispanic origin or not of Hispanic origin. If the respondents are of Hispanic origin they are further asked to indicate the specific Hispanic group (e.g., Cuban, Puerto Rican, Mexican-American, or Other Hispanic) of which they and each other member of the household are a member. Hispanic is not a race category nor does White, Black, etc., refer to an ethnic category. Race and ethnicity are different dimensions derived from responses to different questions.

Rate: A measure of the relative frequency of occurrence of an event in a population.
- **Crude rates** measure the occurrence relative to the total population (see Figure 3.2 and Figure 3.19).
- **General rates** limit the measurement to those age groups of persons in a population actually at risk of the event and is generally computed by dividing the number of occurrences by the number of persons at risk, with the result being multiplied by a constant (usually 1,000) (see Figure 3.3 and Figure 3.19).
- **Specific rates** measure events relative to a specific segment of the population at risk (see Figure 3.4 and Figure 3.19).

Rate Decomposition: A procedure for decomposing the difference between two crude rates of occurrence by using one or another form of weighted average of the composition and the specific rates of the populations being compared to analyze the sources of the differences.

Relationship: The census short form asks for the relationship of each resident in a housing unit to the householder. This question provides data for determining classification of the household as "family" or "nonfamily" as well as providing information on the composition of households.

Residual Net Migration Rate: A net migration rate in which the total amount of population change due to births and deaths is known and the difference between the births/deaths population change and the total population change (the residual) is assumed to be due to migration (see Figure 3.11).

Rule of 70: A popular shorthand for a means of computing the doubling time for a population growing at any given rate. The doubling time is derived by dividing the annual rate of population growth into 70. For example: a 2.0 percent rate of annual growth doubles the population in 35 years.

Rural: see *Urban and Rural*

Segregation Index: see *Index of Dissimilarity*

Service Area: The region applicable for specific service-related actions, policies, or activities.

Sex and Gender: Sex is self identified on the census and most other surveys by marking either "male" or "female. While "sex" refers to a descriptive biological term, the characteristics of men and women referred to as "gender related" (such as differences in occupational distributions and income levels) appear to be the result of social, cultural, and economic differences experienced by males and females.

Sex Ratio: The number of males divided by the number of females and multiplied by 100 (see Figure 3.17).

Single-Decrement Life Table: A life table that only examines the effect of rates of transition from life to death on a population (see Figure 3.8 and Figure 3.9).

Standardization: An analytical technique used to compare two or more populations to determine whether differences among them in the occurrence of an event or phenomenon are due to differences in population characteristics. See Figure 3.20 for examples of direct and indirect standardization.
- **Direct standardization** of two or more populations involves comparing the numbers of occurrences obtained in each population being compared by applying the specific rates for each population to the composition of a standard population
- **Indirect standardization** applies a set of specific rates from a standard population to each of the population compositions of the areas to be compared.
- **Standard population** can refer to any population but usually applies to a larger area of which the areas to be compared are a part, or areas that are similar to the areas being compared. For example, a state may be used as the standard population to compare counties and a county may be used as the standard population to compare cities within it.

State: The primary division of the United States encompassing the 50 states. In census tabulations, the District of Columbia is often treated as an equivalent to a state.

Statistical Geographic Entities: Areas that have been developed and defined for reporting purposes or for data collection and tabulation purposes (for example: census tracts and census blocks) but have no political or governmental functions.

Suburban: The residential area around a major city and the population living in that area. The census does not recognize or use the term "suburb" or "suburban," but suburban is often defined as a county within a Metropolitan Statistical Area outside of the Central City County.

Survey of Income and Program Participation (SIPP): A Census Bureau survey used to measure income-related characteristics and participation in government programs. It records all changes for all household members for a minimum of a 30-month period. It provides the data in the P-70 census publication series.

Survival Rate: A rate computed for a specified population and geographic area indicating the probability that a person will survive from one age to another.

Tenure: This housing characteristic is asked on the census questionnaire for all occupied housing units in order to classify the unit as "owner occupied" or "renter occupied." Tenure data have been collected by the Census Bureau since 1890, though with different details regarding ownership (with or without a mortgage) and rent (with or without cash payment).
- **Owner occupied housing units** are those in which the person completing the questionnaire or someone else who lives in the household owns the housing unit, even if it is mortgaged or in the process of being purchased.
- **Renter occupied housing units** are not occupied by the owner and are classified as "renter occupied" if someone other than the owner occupies the unit whether the unit is rented or occupied without cash rent.

Total Fertility Rate (TFR): The sum of the age-specific fertility rates for all women in the child-bearing ages, and when adjusted to be per-person-specific, indicates the number of children that the average woman would have in her reproductive lifetime if she aged through her reproductive years exposed to the age-specific rates prevailing at a specific point in time (see Figure 3.6).

Tract: see *Census Tract*

Trade Area: The area from which a retail facility consistently draws a majority of its customers, also called a **market area**.

Unemployed Persons: Persons who are not employed but are actively looking for work through a state employment office.

Unemployment Rate*: The percentage of the labor force that is unemployed.

United States: The national geographic level that includes the 50 states and the District of Columbia.

Universe (population): Relevant to a data set, the universe is the entire aggregation of items included.

Urban and Rural: Refers to areas defined by population density. Generally, as of 2000, areas with population densities of 1,000 or more persons per square mile are "urban" and areas with lower densities are "rural." This general definition does not apply to pre-2000 periods.

Urbanized Area (UA): As defined by the Census Bureau following Census 2000, a UA consists of contiguous, densely settled census block groups (BGs) and census blocks that meet minimum population density requirements, along with adjacent densely settled census blocks that together encompass a population of at least 50,000 people.

Urbanized Cluster (UC): As defined by the Census Bureau following Census 2000, a UC consists of contiguous, densely settled census block groups and census blocks that meet minimum population density requirements, along with adjacent densely settled census blocks that together encompass a population of at least 2,500 people but fewer than 50,000 people (U.S. Census Bureau 2002).

Voting Tabulation District (VTD): A generic name for an election district, precinct, or ward.

Wealth: A reference to total asset accumulation. The wealth of a person, household, or family would include savings and the value of goods, property, and possessions that have market value.

Workforce: The sum of the employed and unemployed in an area. Persons who are not able to be employed or are not actively seeking employment are not considered part of the workforce.

Appendix B
Selected Internet Sites for Demographic Data and Communication Resources

Introduction

The information in this appendix is intended as a resource for Internet-based research on demographic and socioeconomic subjects. It first presents a brief overview of Web address naming conventions that should help those less experienced with Internet research to recognize patterns and methods for locating information, and then provides the Web sites for a selected set of agencies, organizations, and other groups.

The specific Web sites provided here are only those that the authors have found useful for a wide range of research purposes. No claim is made that the list is either exhaustive or even comprehensive. It is also important to recognize that sites change names and locations periodically, and, although the sites listed below were verified prior to publication, they are subject to change due to changes in the name of a company, agency, or organization; because it has moved physically and changed its server; or for a variety of other reasons. If the site listed has changed, a search for key words associated with the agency, organization, or group will usually help you locate the new site address.

Names on the Internet

An Internet name (aka: URL or address) is decoded from right to left. The rightmost part of the address is called a top-level domain or a zone. If you are reading a name ending with "com," that is a "commercial" site. The next part of the name is the name of the company. The zone and company may be the entire name needed to get you to a site (for example, http://www.compuserve.com/). If the name is longer, the next item to the left would specify the computer in the company (for example, http:// www.txsdc.utsa.edu/).

In the U.S., *most* Internet sites have names with three-letter zones as listed by organization types below. Elsewhere, names most commonly use geographic zones (some state offices also use geographic zones, for example the Public Utility Commission in Texas is http://www.puc.state.tx.us/).

Zones Based on Organization Type:
.com   Commercial organization
.edu   Educational institution
.gov   Government body or agency
.int   International organization (at the time of this publication, mostly NATO)

.mil   Military site
.net   Networking organization
.org   Nonprofit or noncommercial organization

Zones based on Geographic areas:

AU	Australia	NL	Netherlands (Kingdom of the)
AT	Austria (Republic of)	NO	Norway (Kingdom of)
BE	Belgium (Kingdom of)	RU	Russian Federation
CA	Canada	SU	Former Soviet Union (officially
CZ	Czech Republic		obsolete but still in use)
DK	Denmark (Kingdom of)	ES	Spain (Kingdom of)
FI	Finland (Republic of)	SE	Sweden (Kingdom of)
FR	France (French Republic)	CH	Switzerland (Swiss Confederation)
DE	Germany (Federal Republic of)	TW	Taiwan, Province of China
IN	India (Republic of)	UK	United Kingdom (official code is
IE	Ireland		GB)
IL	Israel (State of)	US	United States (United States of
IT	Italy (Italian Republic)		America)
JP	Japan		

Selected Internet Search Engines:

Agency or Group	Internet Address
Alta Vista	http://www.altavista.com/
Excite	http://travel.excite.com/
Google	http://www.google.com/
EINet Galaxy	http://www.galaxy.com/
GO.com	http://www.go.com/
Lycos	http://www.lycos.com/
Netscape	http://www.netscape.com/
Yahoo	http://www.yahoo.com/
Webcrawler	http://www.webcrawler.com/
MSN Search	http://www.msn.com/
Internet Resources Meta-Index	http://www.ncsa.uiuc.edu/SDG/

Selected Demographic and Statistical Resources for the Press:

Site Description	Internet Address
Australian National University's Internet guide to population and demography	http://demography.anu.edu.au/Virtual Library/

Empire State College's (State University of New York) page of demographic and related links	http://www.esc.edu/esconline/Across_esc/cdl/cdl.nsf/wholeshortlinks2/demography+and+Links?opendocument
Statistical resources on the Web, demographic and housing reports, from the University of Michigan's Document Center	http://www.lib.umich.edu/govdocs/stdemog.html
Statistics.com (Demographic research links)	http://www.statistics.com/

Selected Resources for Journalists:

Site Description	Internet Address
American Press Institute: Writing With Numbers	http://www.americanpressinstitute.org/content/4012.cfm
Project for Excellence In Journalism's "Using Numbers"	http://www.journalism.org/resources/tools/reporting/numbers/print.asp
Power Reporting: Resources for Journalists	http://powerreporting.com/category/Beat_by_beat/Census_2000/
Jeff South's resources for computer-assisted journalism (Virginia Commonwealth University)	http://www.people.vcu.edu/~jcsouth/
Oh, the places journalists should go from Poynter Institute	http://www.poynter.org/content/content_view.asp?id=5180#10
Getting the numbers right, math resources for journalists from NewsLab.org	http://www.newslab.org/resources/math.htm
Numbers in the newsroom from Sarah Cohen of Investigative Reporters and Editors	http://home.earthlink.net/~cassidyny/danger.htm

Demographic Resources and Professional Journals

Resource	Internet Address
American Demographics	http://www.adage.com/section.cms?sectionId=195

Demography: Journal of the Population Association of America	http://www.jstor.org/journals/ 00703370.html
International Migration Review: published by The Center for Migration Studies of New York, Inc.	http://www.jstor.org/journals/ 01979183.html
Population Association of America (PAA)	http://www.popassoc.org/
Population and Development Review: published by the Population Council	http://www.jstor.org/journals/ 00987921.html
Population Council	http://www.popcouncil.org/
Population Index on the Web	http://popindex.princeton.edu/
Population Reference Bureau	http://www.prb.org/

Internet Sites for Governmental and Other National Data Sources:

Agency or Group	Internet Address
Air Force Link	http://www.af.mil/
American Bar Association	http://www.abanet.org/
American Religion Data Archive	http://www.thearda.com/
American Statistical Association	http://www.amstat.org/
Bureau of the Census	http://www.census.gov/
Bureau of Economic Analysis	http://www.bea.gov/
Bureau of Justice Statistics	http://www.ojp.usdoj.gov/bjs/
Bureau of Labor Statistics	http://www.bls.gov/
Bureau of Transportation Statistics	http://www.bts.gov/
Center for Disease Control and Prevention	http://www.cdc.gov/cdc.html
Central Intelligence Agency (CIA)	http://www.cia.gov/ http://www.odci.gov/
Defense Link (U.S. Department of Defense)	http://www.defenselink.mil/

Economic Research Service Department of Agriculture	http://www.ers.usda.gov/
Electronic Embassy	http://www.embassy.org/
Energy Information Administration	http://www.eia.doe.gov/
Environmental Protection Agency	http://www.epa.gov/
Federal Bureau of Investigation (FBI)	http://www.fbi.gov/
Federal Bureau of Prisons	http://www.bop.gov/
Federal Register	http://www.gpoaccess.gov/fr/
Federal Reserve	http://www.federalreserve.gov/
Fed World	http://www.fedworld.gov/
FedStats: The gateway to statistics from U.S. federal agencies	http://www.fedstats.gov/
FirstGov.gov: The U.S. Government's Official Web Portal	http://firstgov.gov/
Government Accountability Office (GAO)	http://www.gao.gov/
Geodata.gov: U.S. Maps and Data	http://www.geodata.gov/
Geospatial and Statistical Data Center - University of Virginia Library	http://fisher.lib.virginia.edu/
Glenmary Research Center: Religious Membership Information	http://www.glenmary.org/grc/ default.htm
Government Printing Office	http://www.access.gpo.gov/
Health and Human Services	http://www.os.dhhs.gov/
Historical Census Browser - University of Virginia Library	http://fisher.lib.virginia.edu/ collections/stats/histcensus/
Internal Revenue Service: Tax Stats	http://www.irs.gov/taxstats/
KIDS COUNT: National and state indicators of child well-being	http://www.aecf.org/kidscount/
Library of Congress	http://www.loc.gov/
National Agricultural Statistics Service	http://www.usda.gov/nass/
National Archives and Records Administration	http://www.nara.gov/

National Center for Education Statistics (NCES)	http://nces.ed.gov/
National Center for Health Statistics (NCHS)	http://www.cdc.gov/nchs/
National Institute of Health	http://www.nih.gov/
National Spatial Data Infrastructure: Geospatial One-Stop	http://www.geo-one-stop.gov/
Navy OnLine	http://www.ncts.navy.mil/
National Oceanic & Atmospheric Administration	http://www.noaa.gov/
Office of Management and Budget (OMB)	http://www.whitehouse.gov/omb/
Science Resources Studies National Science Foundation (NSF)	http://www.nsf.gov/statistics/
Small Business Administration	http://www.sbaonline.sba.gov/
Smithsonian Institution	http://www.si.edu/
Social Security Administration	http://www.ssa.gov/
THOMAS-Legislative Information	http://thomas.loc.gov/
TradeStats Express™ Home	http://tse.export.gov/
U.S. Citizenship and Immigration Services	http://uscis.gov/
U.S. Department of Agriculture	http://www.usda.gov/
U.S. Department of Commerce	http://www.commerce.gov/
U.S. Department of Education	http://www.ed.gov/
U.S. Department of Energy	http://www.doe.gov/
U.S. Department of Housing and Urban Development	http://www.hud.gov/
U.S. Department of the Interior	http://www.doi.gov/
U.S. Department of Justice	http://www.usdoj.gov/
U.S. Department of Labor	http://www.dol.gov/
U.S. Department of Transportation	http://www.dot.gov/
U.S. Fish and Wildlife Service	http://www.fws.gov/

U.S. Geological Survey	http://www.usgs.gov/
U.S. House of Representatives	http://www.house.gov/
U.S. Postal Service	http://www.usps.gov/
U.S. Senate	http://www.senate.gov/
Veterans Affairs	http://www.va.gov/
Virtual Library - Law	http://www.law.indiana.edu/v-lib/
White House Information	http://www.whitehouse.gov/

Selected Internet Sites for State-Level Data Providers by Service Area:

<u>Agency or Group</u>   <u>Internet Address</u>

Population Data

State Data Centers	http://www.census.gov/sdc/www/
The Federal State Cooperative Program for Population Estimates State Contact List	http://www.census.gov/population/ www/coop/contacts.html
The Federal State Cooperative Program for Population Projections State Contact List	http://www.census.gov/population/ www/fscpp/fscpp-contacts.html

Spatial Data

National Spatial Data Infrastructure Geospatial One-Stop State Clearinghouse Web sites	http://www.geo-one-stop.gov/ StateLinks/
USGS - The National Map State Partners	http://nationalmap.gov/partnerships/ state_partners.html

Health Data

National Center for Health Statistics - State Health Departments	http://www.cdc.gov/nchs/about/ major/natality/sites.htm
Behavioral Risk Factor Surveillance System State Contacts	http://www.cdc.gov/brfss/ stateinfo.htm
Behavioral Risk Factor Surveillance System Prevalence Data	http://apps.nccd.cdc.gov/brfss/

State and Local Government on the
Net - State Health Departments and
Services

http://www.statelocalgov.net/
50states-health.cfm

Human Service Data

Centers for Medicare & Medicaid
Services

http://www.cms.hhs.gov/
researchers/statsdata.asp

U.S. Administration on Aging - State
and Area Agencies

http://www.aoa.gov/eldfam/
How_To_Find/Agencies/
Agencies.asp

State and Local Government on the
Net - State Aging Offices

http://www.statelocalgov.net/
50states-aging.cfm

Education Data

U.S. Department of Education - State
Contacts

http://www.ed.gov/about/contacts/
state/

National Center for Education
Statistics - State Education Agencies

http://nces.ed.gov/ccd/ccseas.asp

Agriculture Data

U.S. Department of Agriculture -
Cooperative State Research,
Education, and Extension Service
State and National Partners

http://www.csrees.usda.gov/qlinks/
partners/state_partners.html

State and Local Government on the
Net - State Agricultural Departments

http://www.statelocalgov.net/
50states-agriculture.cfm

Fiscal and Economic Data

The National Association of State
Auditors, Comptrollers and Treasurers

http://www.nasact.org/memberdir/

National Association of State Budget
Officers

http://www.nasbo.org/
directoryPublicDirectory.php

Commerce and Business Data

U.S. Small Business Administration Office of Entrepreneurial Development Office of Small Business Development Centers

http://www.sba.gov/sbdc/sbdcnear.html

Minority Business Development Agency

http://www.mbda.gov/

Labor and Workforce Data

U.S. Department of Labor Employment & Training Administration State Offices of Workforce Security

http://www.workforcesecurity.doleta.gov/map.asp

U.S. Department of Labor Bureau of Labor Statistics U.S. Economy at a Glance

http://www.bls.gov/eag/

State and Local Government on the Net - State Employment Sites and Government Jobs

http://www.statelocalgov.net/50states-jobs.cfm

Criminal Justice Data

www.corrections.com - State Links to Criminal Justice and Correctional Facilities

http://www.corrections.com/links/viewlinks.asp?cat=30

State and Local Government on the Net - Public Safety and Emergency Management

http://www.statelocalgov.net/50states-public-safety.cfm

Transportation Data

National Highway Traffic Safety Administration State Data System

http://www-nrd.nhtsa.dot.gov/departments/nrd-30/ncsa/SDS.html

U.S. Department of Transportation Federal Highway Administration State Transportation Web sites

http://www.fhwa.dot.gov/webstate.htm

| U.S. Department of Transportation Federal Highway Administration State and Local GIS Practices | http://www.gis.fhwa.dot.gov/statepracs.asp |
| State and Local Government on the Net - Transportation and Public Works | http://www.statelocalgov.net/50states-public-works.cfm |

Natural Resource Data

| State and Local Government on the Net - State Parks | http://www.statelocalgov.net/50states-parks.cfm |

Tourism Data

| FirstGov.gov State Travel and Tourism Sites | http://www.firstgov.gov/Citizen/Topics/Travel_Tourism/State_Tourism.shtml |
| State and Local Government on the Net - State Tourism Sites | http://www.statelocalgov.net/50states-tourism.cfm |

Building and Construction Data

| U.S. Census Bureau - Building Permits | http://www.census.gov/const/www/permitsindex.html |
| U.S. Department of Housing and Urban Development | http://www.hud.gov/local/ |

Regulatory Data

| State and Local Government on the Net - State Regulatory Boards and Offices | http://www.statelocalgov.net/50states-regulatory.cfm |

Selected Internet Sites for International Statistical Sources:

Agency or Group	Internet Address
Bangladesh Bureau of Statistics	http://www.bbsgov.org/
Brazilian Institute of Geography and Statistics (IBGE)	http://www.ibge.gov.br/english/default.php

Census and Statistics Department Hong Kong SAR - People's Republic of China	http://www.info.gov.hk/ censtatd/home.html
Census of India	http://www.censusindia.net/
Central Statistics Office Ireland	http://www.cso.ie/
CIA (World Factbook)	http://www.cia.gov/cia/ publications/factbook/index.html
e-Mexico (in English)	http://www.emexico.gob.mx/wb2/ eMex/Home/
France: National Institute for Demographic Studies (INED)	http://www.ined.fr/ englishversion/index.html
France: National Institute of Statistics and Economic Studies (INSEE)	http://www.insee.fr/en/home/home_ page.asp
Germany: Federal Statistical Office Germany	http://www.destatis.de/e_home.htm
International Programs Center (IPC), U.S. Census Bureau	http://www.census.gov/ipc/www/
Instituto National de Estadistica Geographia e Informatica (INEGI) - Mexico's equivalent to the Census Bureau	http://www.inegi.gob.mx/ inegi/default.asp
Japan: Statistics Bureau	http://www.stat.go.jp/english/index. htm
National Bureau of Statistics of China	http://www.stats.gov.cn/ english/index.htm
National Statistics: Home of Official UK Statistics	http://www.statistics.gov.uk/
Russia: Federal State Statistics Service	http://www.gks.ru/eng/
Population Reference Bureau	http://www.prb.org/
Statistics Canada	http://www.statcan.ca/start.html

Statistics Division: Government of Pakistan	http://www.statpak.gov.pk/
Statistics Indonesia Badan Pusat Statistik (BPS)	http://www.bps.go.id/index.shtml
United Nations Population Information Network	http://www.un.org/popin/
United Nations Statistics Division	http://unstats.un.org/unsd/default.htm
World Health Organization	http://www.who.int/en/
World Trade Organization	http://www.wto.org/

References

Chandler, David M., with Bill Kirkner and Jim Minatel. 1995. *Running a Perfect Web Site*. Indianapolis, IN: Que Corporation.

"Guide to the Internet." 1996. *PC Novice*, (4)5. Lincoln, NE: Peed Corporation.

Hoffman, Paul. 1995. *Destination INTERNET and World Wide Web*. Foster City, CA: IDG Books Worldwide Inc.

Kent, Peter. 1994. *The Complete Idiot's Guide to the Internet*. Indianapolis, IN: Alpha Books.

Levine, John R., and Carol Baroudi. 1993. *The Internet for Dummies*. San Mateo, CA: IDG Books.

Vincent, Patrick. 1994. *Free Stuff from the Internet*. Scottsdale, AZ: The Coriolis Group.

Appendix C

How to Work with the Media:
A Guide for Government, Business,
and Demographic Professionals

Lucky you. The boss has just made you the department liaison to the news media. From now on, you'll be taking phone calls from the press.

Prey for the predators? Or opportunities unlimited? Your attitude toward the assignment will go a long way in determining your success at the job.

You will fill the space between the public's right to know and your institution's desire to control publicity about its affairs. If you work for a government agency, freedom of information laws will regulate the process.

But you're a demographer, you say, or work closely with them. The demographic information your agency or business deals with is important but often complicated stuff. The information flow you're called upon to facilitate isn't easy by nature, and the attention span of the press seems shallower and shallower in the age of the 24 by 7 media culture.

So, just how will you navigate the demands of the reporter on deadline and your boss's expectations for positive press?

Following are the demographer's dozen tips for working with the media. Some may seem repetitive, but these guidelines are intended to capture some of the nuances of journalism and spotlight angles that reporters often take in crafting stories using demographic information.

1. Data should be seen, not just heard. In the age of instant, it's more important than ever to put a face behind the voice. Whenever possible, meet face-to-face to do interviews. When you meet with reporters, have a bonus waiting. Have copies of data prepared. Highlight sections of data that show variance—the "what's new about these numbers" angles that interest reporters and editors. Reporters will push to get needed information over the phone under deadline, but try to meet with them in person at the first available opportunity.

2. Do the math. A journalism teacher once described her students as *do-gooders who hate math,* says Deborah Potter, president and executive director of

NewsLab, a nonprofit journalism training and research center in Washington, D.C. An aversion to all things numerical seems universal among journalists, yet reporters and editors are suckers for numbers, she says,

> To them a number looks solid, factual, more trustworthy than a fallible human source. And being numerically incompetent, they can't find the flaws in statistics and calculations. They can't tell the difference between a meaningless number and a significant one. The result is stories that are misleading and confusing at best, and at worst flat out wrong.

Save yourself time and pain. Don't leave journalists to calculate differences, figure percentages, or find the decimal point. Do the math because most reporters are lousy at it.

3.   Explain demographic terms and nuances. When reporters do the math, they usually use words to present it. Make sure they're correctly using those words. Don't assume journalists know the difference between race and ethnicity, migration and immigration, households and families, current dollars and constant dollars, and similar terms. To express relative risks or characterize meaning in numbers, reporters will use terms such as "as likely" or "more likely." Make it likely they will use the terms correctly. Don't be patronizing, but look or listen for a convincing nod of agreement or the voice inflected equivalent. When in doubt, ask: "Do you understand what the term (fill in the blank) means?"

4.   Dance responsibly. Point out trends in the data, but be wary of drawing or being drawn into conclusions that aren't fully supported by the data. Reporters are fond of asking, "So what these numbers mean is (fill in the blank)?" If you answer "yes," make sure you're comfortable seeing your reply in a headline with the sourcing "expert says." Bottom line: simply convey what your demographic data show, tell how they're different from previous data, and explain what, if any, implications or applications the data might have. Be sure to explain data caveats precisely.

5.   Trend at your own risk. Be wary of using the journalist's favorite demographic term "trend." In most newsrooms, a trend is something that has happened two or more times. If your data support a trend, be prepared to discuss it from all angles. The only person who likes trends more than a reporter is the reporter's boss.

6.   Push back. If pressed for conclusions, or analyses of data, that can't be supported by the data, say that. "I can't draw such a conclusion from these data." If there are areas of further analyses that need to be done before you can offer further judgments that might help the reporter, say that. "I can't say what this means because we haven't had a chance to analyze all the data, compare it, or contrast it with previous work. I know you understand that because you face similar challenges all the time." If it is a hot story, acknowledge the interest level. "You're posing some good questions. We hope to have some additional information when we dig into the numbers a little more." This is the quote that likely will end up in the newspaper or on TV.

7.   If you don't know the answer, that's okay. When you don't have the information needed by a reporter, just say so. If you can get it before the reporter's deadline, tell the reporter you'll get the information to him or her. Send the information by e-mail or fax and keep a copy on file. Reporters deal all day long with unanswered questions, so they'll understand when you don't know the answer to one of their queries.

8.   Beware of becoming Joe and Suzy Sixpack. Good reporters will attempt to put a face behind the numbers in their stories. Reporters, especially those in smaller media markets, are under pressure to turn in at least one story a day. In the rush to meet deadlines, they'll often make the officials they're writing about "the face" behind the numbers. You may be the expert who provides the data, but you're not a good example of the data. Reporters may seek your advice on where to find people for their stories, but that's really not your job to provide. Urge them to seek out colleagues for ideas. If you offer an example of a "face," be prepared to see it in print or on TV with your name attached as the source.

9.   The demographer's challenge: trusting the reporter to get it right. No, you can't read the reporter's story or proof the graphics before they're published or broadcast. You may and should expect, however, that the reporter understands the data you have provided. If you know the story to be particularly complex, offer help right up until the story is published. "If you have any further questions, please don't hesitate to e-mail or phone me." The smartest reporters will seek you out in advance of their deadlines and carefully review their stories to ensure accuracy and clarity.

10. Don't engage in the crossfire unless you can bear being wounded. Some agenda-driven groups routinely use (or misuse) data to further their causes. The responsible press attempts to independently verify claims of such data before reporting it, but in the nonstop rush to feed the round-the-clock news cycle, the verification may not happen. In some of these cases, government and business

must respond to agenda-driven groups by setting the record straight. It is always tempting to do so. Some reporters won't think twice about calling demographers unaffiliated with the case, seeking an outside "objective" view of the facts. Unless you are intimately familiar with the subject at hand, avoid getting caught in this trap. You will be used to either knock down or affirm the data—a position that could compromise your credibility.

11. Confront media mistakes. If a journalist, regardless of medium, screwed up using the demographic data you provided, missed the story altogether, or, as is more often the case, told a story that the numbers don't support, confront the journalist directly. Tell him or her of the error and that it needs to be corrected in the next newscast or the next edition of the newspaper. If you contributed to the error in some way, acknowledge your role in the mistake. Do not go to the reporter's editor unless there is a repeated and documented pattern of errors. In respectable journalism, two errors is a pattern. In legitimate newsrooms, correcting the errors of reporters and editors is serious business. Many newsrooms have sophisticated databases that track errors and who made them. When reporting an error, make sure your expectation for a correction is clear. "Where and when will I read this correction in the newspaper? How will you report the correction?" On the other hand, if a correction isn't required, say that. "This is a quibble. A correction isn't required, but I wanted to follow up with you to make sure you understood the full definition of the term."

12. Praise good work. We all like to hear that we're doing a good job. If a journalist has accurately and fairly reflected the importance of data in a story, drop her or him a note. Better yet, if the reporter's beat involves regular contact, you can develop a professional working relationship that helps both of you develop your skills and craft.

Finally, don't categorize all reporters as the same. While journalists do not constitute a representative sample of the U.S. population—indeed, the educational and income levels of reporters and editors at major media outlets are higher than the national average and their politics tend to be more liberal than those of the average American—they are not all that different from other professionals.

While they will make mistakes—just like any good demographer—most reporters also work diligently to provide citizens with the information they need to be free and self-governing (just like any good demographer).

Appendix D

How to Work with Professional Demographers in Government, Academia, and Business: A Guide for News Media Professionals

In their book, *The Elements of Journalism* (2001), authors Bill Kovach and Tom Rosentiel say the primary purpose of journalism is to provide citizens with information needed to be free and self-governing. They believe:

- Journalism's first obligation is to truth;
- Journalism's first loyalty is to citizens;
- The essence of journalism is a discipline of verification;
- Journalists must maintain an independence from those that they cover;
- Journalists must serve as independent monitors of power;
- Journalism must provide a forum for public criticism and comment;
- Journalists must make the significant interesting and relevant; and
- Journalists should keep the news in proportion and make it comprehensive.

These values are similar—some are identical—to those championed by demographic professionals around the globe. Serving the public's interest with truthful information that has been verified, nuanced, and made public in relevant ways is the job description of most professional demographers.

Indeed, value differences aren't the main source of friction between demographers and those in the press who work closely with them; the conflict arises over expectations.

Generally speaking, two rules govern the expectations of professionals who regularly work with journalists: know your subject[1] and be fair.

Rule No. 1: Know Your Subject.

The first rule should go without saying, but it must be repeated, as the careers of Jay Leno, David Letterman, and Jon Stewart attest. Credibility starts with journalists knowing their subject.

"No amount of writing skill or tricks for simplification will succeed unless you know what you're talking or writing about," says Tom Siegfried, the award-winning science writer and editor for many years at *The Dallas Morning News.* "You have to know the background to the story, the history, the scientific principles of whatever field it is you're writing about. If you don't know these things, you need to find them out."

Nothing drives a demographer (or any professional, for that matter) battier than a reporter who doesn't know the subject matter that he or she purportedly is going to tell people the truth about.

William Dunn (1992:190–191), author of *Selling The Story: The Layman's Guide to Collecting and Communicating Demographic Information,* notes that the unrelenting pressure to produce news stories to fill the news hole and air time is a problem for reporters.

> The fact of the matter is: news articles, particularly those written on tight deadlines, are often incomplete, imprecise and sometimes contain errors. The correction columns in newspapers and magazines are the proof. There are often sweeping generalizations drawn from specific cases, exaggeration and use of inappropriate data to quantify something.

In working with demographers, journalists should know the basic principles of demography—the variables of population size and change, mortality, fertility, and migration (national and international); the geographic boundary definitions for metropolitan and nonmetropolitan areas, central cities and suburbs, rural and urban areas (by the population size, density of settlement, and among blocks, tracts, etc. of an area); and the compositional characteristics (from age, gender, and race and ethnicity to household and family types, educational status, employment, wealth and poverty).

Journalists should know how to handle these often complex terms and the numbers generated by them.

Let's face the painful truth: journalists are terrible with math. MathMistakes.com, a Web site devoted to the miscalculations made over and over by the media and others, is ample proof.

A few examples of the comical (but sad) entries by creator Paul Cox and contributors:

Dramadigits. The reporting of a number with more significant digits than what can be reasonably expected. *Ivory soap loves to brag that it is 99.44 percent pure. It is impossible that each bar is exactly that pure. How do they get away with it? The 99.44 percent pure statement is a trademark, not a statement of fact.*

Raw number. The reporting of an "impressive" number that is meaningless without something to compare it to. *Example: every day cars in America produce over a billion tons of pollution. That may be an impressive statement, but it is meaningless without something to compare it to. A better statistic is that cars are responsible for more than half of the carbon monoxide pollution.*

Shooting the barn statistics. A story is told about a Texas sharpshooter who shot his gun into the side of a barn 30 times, then painted a circle around where most of the bullets landed, calling that his target. Collecting statistical data without first knowing what you are looking for results in bad statistics.

Reporters need to develop "math intuition" so they can tell when the numbers they're looking at just don't add up, said Deborah Potter, president and executive director of NewsLab, a nonprofit journalism training and research center in Washington, D.C. *They need math mechanics to find the meaning behind figures and data. Simply put, journalists need to make sense of numbers the way they need language skills to make sense of words.*

> The old worry that you can know too much about a subject to communicate it clearly is nonsense. True, you have to guard against forgetting how much your audience does not know once you've learned about a subject. But the only way you will be able to communicate complex subject matter clearly is to understand it first yourself (Siegfried 1998).

Rule No. 2: Be Fair.

A common complaint among demographers is the misuse of information—the intentional manipulation of data, and its shading and tone, in support of a story thesis. This is the complaint of "unfairness."

Kovach and Rosentiel (2001:77) point out the inherent difficulties with fairness—that it's too abstract to define, and more subjective than truth. "Fair to whom?" they ask. "How do you test fairness?"

Fairness should mean the journalist is being fair to the facts, and to a citizen's understanding of them. It should not mean, "Am I being fair to my sources, so that none of them will be unhappy?" the authors write.

They propose a core set of concepts—what they call the "intellectual principles of a science of reporting"—that forms "the foundation of the discipline of verification" and eliminates questions of fairness.

The principles are:

1. Never add anything that was not there. "Do not add" means do not add things that did not happen. This admonition goes further than "never invent or make things up," for it also encompasses rearranging events in time or place or conflating characters or events.
2. Never deceive the audience. "Do not deceive" means never mislead the audience. *Fooling people is a form of lying and mocks the idea that journalism is committed to truthfulness.*
3. Be as transparent as possible about your methods and motives. *How do you know what you know? Who are your sources? How direct is their knowledge? What biases might they have? Are there conflicting accounts? What don't we know?*
4. Rely on your own original reporting. Too often, reporters merely pick up the work of competitors without even attempting to independently verify the truthfulness of the story.
5. Exercise humility. Journalists should not only be skeptical of what they see and hear from others, but just as importantly, *they should be skeptical about their ability to know what it really means. A key way to avoid misrepresenting events is a disciplined honesty about the limits of one's knowledge and the power of one's perception.*

A focus on synthesis and verification—a concentration on what is true and important about a story—is the best antidote to the rumor, innuendo, the insignificant, and spin that feed today's new journalism of assertion, the authors argue.

Indeed, so-called "editorializing" is a common complaint made against journalists. Dunn (1992:191) said it boils down to a matter of shading and tone.

> Most journalists strive for objectivity. But some others, practicing what used to be called 'new journalism,' believe in having a point of view and taking an advocacy stance, which can lead to the highlighting of one set of factors or statistics over another. That's certainly the case with many columnists, especially in the editorial pages.

Daniel Okrent, public editor of the *New York Times*, wrote in a 2004 column that *Fairness requires the consideration of all sides of an issue; it doesn't require the uncritical reporting of any.* He suggests a middle ground in the ongoing arm-wrestling over "objectivity" in the media culture of 24-hour news.

> *I'm not calling for unsupported opinion, but for a flowering of the facts—not just those recorded stenographically or uttered by experts, but the sort that arise from experience, knowledge and a brave willingness to stand behind what you know to be true.*

---

1   Definitions of commonly used demographic terms are provided in Appendix A. A list of selected Internet sites on demographic data is provided in Appendix B.

References

Bass, Frank. 2001. *The Associated Press Guide to Internet Research and Reporting*. Cambridge, MA: Perseus Publishing.

Bean, F.D., A.G. King, R.D. Benford, and L.B. Perkinson. 1982. *Estimates of the Number of Illegal Migrants in the State of Texas*. Austin: University of Texas Population Research Center.

Bean, F.D., A.G. King, and J.S. Passel. 1983. "The number of illegal migrants of Mexican origin in the United States: sex ratio-based estimators for 1980." *Demography* 20:99-109.

Bianchi, S.M., and N. Rytina. 1986. "The decline in occupational sex segregation during the 1970s: census and CPS comparisons." *Demography* 23:79–86.

Blundell, William. 1988. *The Art and Craft of Feature Writing*. New York: Penguin Books.

Bogue, Donald J. 1968. *Principles of Demography*. New York: John Wiley and Sons.

Brookings Institution. 2003. *Stunning Progress, Hidden Problems: Declines in Concentrated Poverty in the 1990s*. Washington, DC. Transcript of a forum co-sponsored by Brookings.

Buss, Tim, and Karen Davis. 2003. *The Design Trinity*. Dallas: Belo Interactive Inc. Web design guide for employees of Belo Interactive.

Chandler, David M., with Bill Kirkner and Jim Minatel. 1995. *Running a Perfect Web Site*. Indianapolis, IN: Que Corporation.

Clogg, C.C., and S.R. Eliason. 1988. "A flexible procedure for adjusting rates and proportions, including statistical methods for group comparisons." *American Sociological Review* 2:267–283.

Cohen, Sara. 2001. *Danger! Numbers in the Newsroom*. A collection of handouts used in various forms for Investigative Reporters and Editors conferences.

Covey, Franklin. 1999. Style *Guide for Business and Technical Communication*. 3rd ed. Salt Lake City: Franklin Covey Co.

Cox, Paul. *Mathmistakes.com.* Web site devoted to math mistakes made repeatedly by advertisers, the media, reporters, politicians, and activists.

Das Gupta, P. 1978. "A general method of decomposing a difference between two rates into several components." *Demography* 15:99–112.

_____. 1990. Decomposition of the difference between two rates when the factors are nonmultiplicative with applications to U.S. Life Tables. Paper presented at the annual meeting of the Population Association of America. Toronto.

Dietz, John K., Judge, 250th Texas State District Court. 2004. Remarks made before ruling in Texas school finance lawsuit.

Doig, Steve. *Reporting Census 2000: A Guide for Journalists.* (http://cronkite.pp.asu.edu:16080/census/). Web site devoted to helping journalists cover Census 2000. Tempe: Arizona State University.

Draper, N.P., and H. Smith. 1998. *Applied Regression Analysis.* 3rd ed. Wiley: New York.

Dunn, William. 1992. *Selling the Story: The Layman's Guide to Collecting and Communicating Demographic Information.* Ithaca, NY: American Demographics Books.

El Nasser, Haya. "2030 forecast: mostly gray." *USA Today.* April 21, 2005 .

Fossett, M.A., and K.J. Kiecolt. 1990. "Mate availability, family formation, and family structure among Black Americans in nonmetropolitan Louisiana 1970–1980." *Rural Sociology* 55:305–327.

"Guide to the Internet." 1996. *PC Novice*, 4(5). Lincoln, NE: Peed Corporation.

Hart, Jack. *News by the numbers.* http://www.notrain-nogain.org/Default.asp. Training handout for journalists, found at No Train, No Gain, a Web site specializing in training for newspaper journalists.

Hoffman, Paul. 1995. *Destination INTERNET and World Wide Web.* Foster City, CA: IDG Books Worldwide Inc.

Jargowsky, Paul A. 1997. *Poverty and Place: Ghettos, Barrios, and the American City.* New York: Russell Sage Foundation. See also his Web site on urban poverty, http://www.urbanpoverty.net/.

Kelley, Chris. "Population study projects troubling future for Texas." *The Dallas Morning News.* July 28, 1996, A-1.

Kent, Peter. 1994. *The Complete Idiot's Guide to the Internet.* Indianapolis, IN: Alpha Books.

Kintner, Hallie J., 2004. "The Life Table." in *The Methods and Materials of Demography*, Jacob S. Siegel and David A. Swanson, eds. Chapter 13. San Diego: Elsevier Academic Press.

Kintner, Hallie J., Thomas W. Merrick, and Paul R. Voss. 1995. *Demographics: A Casebook.* Boulder, CO: Westview Press.

Kitagawa, E.M. 1955. "Components of a difference between two rates." *Journal of the American Statistical Association* 50:1168–1194.

Kovach, Bill, and Tom Rosentiel. 2001. *The Elements of Journalism: What Newspeople Should Know and the Public Should Expect.* New York: Random House.

Land, K.C., and A. Rogers, eds. 1982. *Multidimensional Mathematical Demography.* New York: Academic Press.

LaRocque, Paula. 1990. *A Dozen Guidelines to Clearer Writing.* Handout at an employee training event at the *Dallas Morning News.*

Lazer, William. 1997. *Handbook of Demographics for Marketing and Advertising: New trends in the American Marketplace.* Landham, MD: Lexington Books.

Levine, John R., and Carol Baroudi. 1993. *The Internet for Dummies.* San Mateo, CA: IDG Books.

Liao, T.F. 1989. "A flexible approach for the decomposition of rate differences." *Demography* 4:717–726.

Lichter, D.T. 1989. "Race, employment hardship, and inequality in the American nonmetropolitan South." *American Sociological Review* 3:436–446.

Lichter, D.T., and J.A. Constanzo. 1987. "Nonmetropolitan underemployment and labor-force composition." *Rural Sociology* 3:329–344.

Lippman, Walter. 1965. *Public Opinion*. paperback ed. New York: Free Press. 216. First pub., 1922.

MacCluggage, Reid. 1998. *Edit more Skeptically*. Anaheim, CA. Speech and handout delivered at the annual convention of the Associated Press Managing Editors.

McFall, Joseph A., Jr. 2003. *Population: A Lively Introduction*. Washington, DC: Population Reference Bureau.

McGehee, Mary A., 2004. "Mortality." in *The Methods and Materials of Demography*, Jacob S. Siegel and David A. Swanson, eds. Chapter 12. San Diego: Elsevier Academic Press.

Massey, D.S., and N.A. Denton. 1988. "The dimensions of residential segregation." *Social Forces* 2:281–315.

Meyer, Philip. 1972. *Precision Journalism: A Reporter's Introduction to Social Science Methods. Bloomington and London*: Indiana University Press.

_____. 1991. *The New Precision Journalism*. Bloomington and Indianapolis: Indiana University Press.

Moreno, Sylvia. "Flow of illegal immigrants to U.S. unabated." *Washington Post*. March 22, 2005. A-2.

Murdock, Steve H., and David R. Ellis. 1991. *Applied Demography: An Introduction to Basic Concepts, Methods, and Data*. Boulder, CO: Westview Press.

Murdock, Steve H., Md. Nazrul Hoque, Martha Michael, Steve White, and Beverly Pecotte. 1997. *The Texas Challenge: Population Change and the Future of Texas*. College Station: Texas A&M University Press.

Murdock, Steve H., Steve White, Md. Nazrul Hoque, Beverly Pecotte, Xuihong You, and Jennifer Balkan. 2003. *The New Texas Challenge: Population Change and the Future of Texas*. College Station: Texas A&M University Press.

Namboodiri, K., and C.M. Suchindran. 1987. *Life Table Techniques and Their Applications*. Orlando: Harcourt, Brace, and Jovanovich.

Nathanson, C.A., and Y.J. Kim. 1989. "Components of change in adolescent fertility." *Demography* 26:85–98.

National Academy of Sciences. 1980. *Estimating Population and Income of Small Areas*. Washington, DC: National Academy Press.

Nielsen, Jakob. 2005. http://www.useit.com/. Web site for useable information technology.

Niles, Robert. http://www.robertniles.com/. Web site with tutorials showing journalists how to use math and data.

Office of Management and Budget. "Standards for Defining Metropolitan and Micropolitan Statistical Areas; Notice." *Federal Register*. 65(249). Wednesday, December 27, 2000.

_____. "Subject: Revised Definitions of Metropolitan Statistical Areas and Combined Statistical Areas, and Guidance on Uses of the Statistical Definitions of These Areas." OMB Bulletin No. 03-04. June 6, 2003.

_____. "Subject: Update of Statistical Area Definitions and Guidance on Their Uses." OMB Bulletin No. 05-02. February 22, 2005.

O'Hare, William P., Kelvin M. Polland, and Amy R. Ritualo. 2004. "Educational and Economic Characteristics " in *The Methods and Materials of Demography*, Jacob S. Siegel and David A. Swanson, eds. Chapter 10. San Diego: Elsevier Academic Press.

Okrent, Daniel. "It's Good to Be Objective. It's Even Better to Be Right." *The New York Times*. Nov. 14, 2004.

Passel, Jeffrey S. 2005. "Estimates of the size and characteristics of the undocumented population." Washington, DC: Pew Hispanic Center.

Pear, Robert. "Smaller percentage of poor living in high-poverty areas." *The New York Times*. May 18, 2003, 26.

Pol, Louis G., and Richard K. Thomas. 1997. *Demography for Business Decision Making*. Westport, CT: Greenwood Publishing Group Inc.

Pollard, A.H., F. Yusuf, and G.N. Pollard. 1990. *Demographic Techniques*. New York: Pergamon Press.

Pooler, James A. 2002. *Demographic Targeting: The Essential Role of Population Groups in Retail Marketing*. Burlington, VT: Ashgate Publishing Company.

Population Reference Bureau. 1998. *PRB's Population Handbook, 4th International Edition.* Washington, DC: Population Reference Bureau.

Potter, Deborah. 2004. "Graphics can make the complex clear." Washington, DC: Newslab.org.

Roberts, Sam. 1994. *Who We Are, a Portrait of America.* New York: Times Books.

Scanlan, Chip. 2003. *Avoiding Number Novocain: Writing Well with Numbers.* www.poynter.org. St. Petersburg, FL.

Shedden, David. 2004. *Tip sheets: design/graphics.* www.poynter.org. St. Petersburg, FL.

Shryock, H., and J. Siegel. 1980. *The Methods and Materials of Demography.* Washington, DC: U. S. Government Printing Office.

Siegel, Jacob S. 2002. *Applied Demography: Applications to Business, Government, Law and Public Policy.* San Diego: Academic Press

Siegel, Jacob S., and David A. Swanson, eds. 2004. *The Methods and Materials of Demography.* San Diego: Elsevier Academic Press.

Siegfried, Tom. 1995. "Clarifying complexity." Handout at an employee training event at the *Dallas Morning News.*

_____. 1998. "Assessing credibility and evaluating evidence." Handout at an employee training event at the *Dallas Morning News*; personal interview.

Smith, Stanley K., Jeff Tayman, and David A. Swanson. 2001. *State and Local Population Projections: Methodology and Analysis.* New York: Kluwer Academic/Plenum Publishers.

Snedecor, G.W., and W.G. Cochran. 1989. *Statistical Methods.* 8th ed. Ames: Iowa State University Press.

Stewart, Ian. 1987. *The Problems of Mathematics.* Oxford: Oxford University Press.

Sweet, J.A. 1984. "Components of change in migration and destination-propensity rates for metropolitan and nonmetropolitan areas: 1935–1980." *Demography* 21:129–140.

The Associated Press. 1999. *AP Stylebook*. New York: The Associated Press.

Tsui, Anne S., and Barbara A. Gutek. 2000. *Demographic Differences in Organizations: Current Research and Future Directions.* Lanham, MD: Lexington Books.

U.S. Bureau of the Census. June 2000. Current Population Survey. Washington, DC: U.S. Bureau of the Census.

_____. "Urban Area Criteria for Census 2000." *Federal Register.* (67)51. Friday, March 15, 2002.

_____. http://www.census.gov/Press-Release/www/releases/. Washington, DC: U.S. Bureau of the Census.

_____. http://www.census.gov/main/www/popclock.html. Washington, DC: U.S. Bureau of the Census.

Vincent, Patrick. 1994. *Free Stuff from the Internet*. Scottsdale, AZ: The Coriolis Group.

Weeks, John R. 2005. *Population: An Introduction to Concepts and Issues*. 9th ed. Belmont, CA: Wadsworth/Thomson Learning.

Weinberg, Steve. 1996. *The Reporter's Handbook: An Investigator's Guide to Documents and Techniques.* New York: St. Martin's Press.

Wilson, F.D. 1988. "Components of change in migration and destination-propensity rates for metropolitan and nonmetropolitan areas: 1935–1980." *Demography* 25:129–139.

Index

185

About the Authors

Dr. Steve Murdock holds the Lutcher Brown Distinguished Chair at The University of Texas at San Antonio and is the State Demographer of Texas. He is the author of eleven books, more than eighty refereed articles, and more than 100 research reports describing the extent and socioeconomic implications of demographic change. His publications include a book on applied demography as well as works on the implications of demographic change for the U.S. and Texas. He is a popular lecturer on demographics and its use and implications to more than ninety public and professional (nonstudent) audiences per year. He is among the most widely quoted academics in the Southwest and was named one of the twenty-five most influential Texans by Texas Monthly in 2005. He teaches courses in demography and statistics and guest lectures in numerous business areas.

Mr. Chris Kelley is editor of DallasNews.com, the Web site of *The Dallas Morning News*. A twenty-six year veteran of the *News*, he has experience as a reporter, editor, and director of multimedia product development. As a reporter for eighteen years, he specialized in writing on demographics. He is thoroughly familiar with the sources, context, and general approach used by members of the press in reporting on demographics. He is equally schooled in practices, problems, and general approaches used by government, business, and demographic professionals who deal with members of the press as part of their jobs. In his current capacity, he has developed expertise on how to effectively use the Internet to locate, analyze, and present demographic information.

Dr. Jeffrey Jordan is a psychologist with research experience in a variety of areas related to the text and with expertise in Web-based data products and services. He is the Web Master for the Texas State Data Center and has worked extensively in the location of Web-based data sources and the appropriate use of data from such sources.

Ms. Beverly Pecotte has served as the Director of Data Services for the Texas State Data Center for more than twenty years. She has extensive experience with data users from the public and private sectors and with members of the media. She has wide-ranging knowledge of federal and state data sources in the areas of population, housing, public services, health, education, labor, and numerous other areas.

Dr. Alvin Luedke is an Associate Professor of Rural Ministry at Luther Seminary in St. Paul, Minnesota. He has a Ph.D in demography and has worked extensively with programs that provide demographic and related information to general public audiences and that teach clergy and institutional and community planners how to obtain and use demographic data for need assessments, site location, marketing, public information dissemination, and related issues.